# BASIC CHINESE GRAMMAR AND SENTENCE PATTERNS

Other Chinese language material published by Wild Peony:

*Putonghua: A Practical Course in Spoken Chinese*
*Mabel Lee and Zhang Wu-ai*

*Readings in Modern Chinese*
*Liu Wei-ping, Mabel Lee, A. J. Prince, Lily Shaw Lee and R. S. W. Hsu*

# BASIC CHINESE GRAMMAR AND SENTENCE PATTERNS

A. D. Syrokomla-Stefanowska
Mabel Lee

wild peony

Published by WILD PEONY PTY LTD
PO Box 636 Broadway NSW 2007 NSW Australia

*First Printed 1986*
*1ˢᵗ Reprint    1989*
*2ⁿᵈ Reprint   1992*
*3ʳᵈ Reprint   2002*

National Library of Australia
Cataloguing-in-Publication entry
Syrokomla-Stefanowska, A. D. (Agnieszka D.).
  Basic Chinese grammar & sentence patterns.
  ISBN 0 9590735 1 5.
  1. Chinese language – Modern Chinese,
  1919–      –Grammar. 2. Chinese language –
  Modern Chinese, 1919 –     –Sentences.
  I. Lee, Mabel. II. Title.
495.15

*Cover design by Paul Soady*
*Set in Times Roman by Frontier Technology, Sydney*
*Printed in Australia by* National Capital Printing, Fyshwick

1-1699

# CONTENTS

# PREFACE

This work is designed for students wishing to establish a solid grounding in the basic grammatical structures and vocabulary of the modern Chinese language with a view to reading modern Chinese literary works and other writings. A pre-publication version has been in use in the Department of Oriental Studies at the University of Sydney since 1981. A growing demand for the work finally encouraged the authors to revise the work and to prepare it for publication. Associate Professor Lu Zengpu of the Beijing Languages Institute checked the manuscript against present-day language norms and usage; Dr Raymond Hsu and Mr Steven Brent examined it meticulously and rigorously in the light of their linguistic expertise. We acknowledge here with gratitude and thanks their valuable assistance.

A. D. Syrokomla-Stefanowska

Mabel Lee

Department of Oriental Studies,
University of Sydney,

March 1986

# INTRODUCTION

The languages of the world have evolved through the ages as a means of human communication. Natural environment has shaped cultural groups and their social organization, customs and traditions. Traits in the thinking of each cultural group led to differences in the inherent organization of languages. However, initially, the evolution of all languages stems from the gradual appearance of discernible and logical patterns in utterances which were imitated and thus reinforced and finally adopted by members of a group. As civilizations developed, the written representation of spoken languages emerged to record speech for posterity, permitting further development in languages and enabling mankind to express thinking of a highly complex nature.

For the effective learning of a foreign language, adult beginners too must be able to discern patterns in the language chosen for study. While rote learning plays a significant role in the language acquistion of small children, for the adult learner, knowledge of the structures and patterns of the new language is essential and rote learning, while still important, plays a lesser role. Knowledge of the patterns used in the organization of the words of a language will provide adult learners with a framework for using vocabulary as it is gradually acquired.

In this book we have attempted to strip the Chinese language down to a skeletal framework, isolating for the English speaker the structures and patterns which are essential and basic in the Chinese language. We have introduced a vocabulary of words which have a high frequency in written Chinese and we have introduced these in blocks of associated words. It is generally agreed that the written language tends to be less verbose and repetitious than speech for in writing one has more time for better organization of thinking; in speech also there is the tendency to omit words when responding in a known context. As many of the expressions common to everday speech do not have a high frequency in written Chinese some of these have not been introduced here. It is recommended that English-speaking beginners of the Chinese language simultaneously work through a course such as **Putonghua: A Practical Course in Spoken Chinese by Mabel Lee & Zhang Wu-ai (Wild Peony, Sydney, 1984)** to gain spoken fluency in Chinese in a Western environment and then follow up with the various books on conversational Chinese in a Beijing setting published in Beijing.

Because of cultural differences, sometimes apparently simple expressions will defy exact translation into another language. We have tried to explain the Chinese language from the point of view of an enquiring adult mind which demands to know why and tries to discern differences in shades of meaning implicit in the different patterns adopted for use under different circumstances. It is knowledge of this kind based on an understanding of the thinking behind the organization of words, which makes for permanence and depth in the learning of a foreign language, and it is this kind of knowledge which will constitute the more solid foundation for development and extension of knowledge and facility of use of a foreign language.

### The Chinese Sentence

Generally the sentence in Chinese follows the pattern SUBJECT + PREDICATE, where the subject may be defined as topic for discussion and the predicate as comment on the topic. This definition is much wider than the more common definiton of actor (subject) and action (predicate). While the definition actor and action will in many cases apply in Chinese, in possibly an equal number of cases it will be seen that a subject plus predicate will translate naturally into the English passive, hence there is a preference for the definition of topic and comment.

An important principle in Chinese, a principle that has applied throughout the history of the Chinese language is that the qualifier must stand before the words qualified. Thus adjectives, possessives, numerals, classifiers and relative clauses precede the nominal and all adverbs and adverbial phrases precede the verb.

Definite and indefinite reference generally depends on position in the sentence; elements standing at the beginning of the sentence are more definite than those standing at the end of the sentence. Thus the subject (the topic for discussion) is definite and the object (part of the predicate or comment on the topic) is indefinite. One may however transpose the object to the position of topical subject in front of the grammatical subject and this has the effect of making the object definite.

A final point to observe is that the minimal answer to questions which in English would be answered with "yes" or "no" is usually the main verb, the auxiliary verb or the preposition; answers to other types of questions, as in English, can consist of a noun only.

*Spelling Conventions Adopted in This Book*
*The system of romanization used is Hanyu Pinyin and generally the conventions for spelling and word boundaries follow those used in* **Elementary Chinese** *(Beijing Languages Institute, Beijing, 1975). It is recommended that beginners first familiarize themselves with Hanyu Pinyin and the sounds and tones of Chinese by referring to the first 6 lessons of this work and the tapes accompanying it. In addition, the following points regarding tones should be observed:*

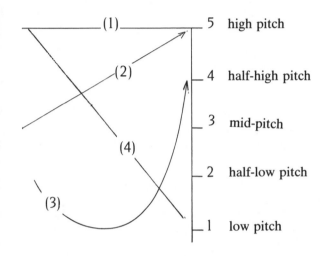

| | | |
|---|---|---|
| 1st tone | e.g. mā | 55 |
| 2nd tone | e.g. má | 35 |
| 3rd tone | e.g. mǎ | 214 |
| 4th tone | e.g. mà | 51 |

1. Tones are indicated with stress marks over the vowel of each syllable (see diagram above); in the case of diphthongs or triphthongs, over the most audible vowel. Syllables pronounced in the neutral tone do not bear a tone mark.

2. Words pronounced in the neutral tone are pronounced quickly and lightly. Particles and suffixes are usually pronounced in the neutral tone. In polysyllabic words, the second syllable may be pronounced in the neutral tone. Words which are usually pronounced with a tone may become neutral in tone when used in particular grammatical structures, e.g. shi 是 loses its tone when used in equative sentences unless strong emphasis is intended,

the negative alternative in an alternative type question pattern is generally pronounced in the neutral tone and personal pronouns used as objects of verbs are also often pronounced in the neutral tone.

3. Third tones are generally pronounced as half-third tones when they are followed by 1st, 2nd, 4th and neutral tone syllables. The third tone falls and rises in pitch i.e. 214 while the half-third tone drops from 2 to 1 in pitch but does not have the final rise of the third tone.

4. When a third tone is followed by another third tone syllable, the first third tone is pronounced as a second tone, e.g. lǐxiǎng (ideal).

5. When a fourth tone syllable is followed by another fourth tone syllable, the first of these only falls to mid-pitch i.e. 53, e.g jìnbù (progress).

6. The neutral tone is influenced by the tone of the preceding syllable. Thus it is pronounced with a half-low pitch when following a first tone (zhīdao, to know); with a midpitch when following a second tone (shénme, what); with a half-high pitch when following a third tone (ěrduo, ear); with a low pitch when following a fourth tone (bàba, father).

7. The tone changes mentioned in 3 to 6 above are not indicated as these changes occur naturally and are consistent changes; the original tone marks are therefore given. However, when a third tone syllable is followed by another third tone syllable which has become a neutral tone, in some words the first third tone syllable is pronounced in second tone. In such cases the tone change is indicated, e.g. láoshu (rat) and kéyi(may). In other words the first third tone will of course be pronounced in the half-third tone as indicated in 6 above.

**LESSON ONE**

# VOCABULARY

| | | | | |
|---|---|---|---|---|
| 1. | guójiā | 國家 | 国家 | nation, country (cl. *ge* 個) |
| 2. | Zhōngguó | 中國 | 中国 | China |
| 3. | Rìběn | 日本 | | Japan |
| 4. | Yīngguó | 英國 | 英国 | England |
| 5. | Fǎguó | 法國 | 法国 | France |
| 6. | Měiguó | 美國 | 美国 | America |
| 7. | Àodàlìyà | 澳大利亞 | 澳大利亚 | Australia |
| 8. | rén | 人 | | person |
| 9. | Zhōngguórén | 中國人 | 中国人 | Chinese (person) |
| 10. | Rìběnrén | 日本人 | | Japanese (person) |
| 11. | Yīngguórén | 英國人 | 英国人 | English (person) |
| 12. | Fǎguórén | 法國人 | 法国人 | French (person) |
| 13. | Měiguórén | 美國人 | 美国人 | American (person) |
| 14. | Àodàlìyàrén | 澳大利亞人 | 澳大利亚人 | Australian (person) |
| 15. | wǒ | 我 | | I |
| 16. | nǐ | 你 | | you |
| 17. | tā | 他 | | he |
| 18. | tā | 她 | | she |
| 19. | wǒmen | 我們 | 我们 | we |
| 20. | nǐmen | 你們 | 你们 | you (plural) |
| 21. | tāmen | 他們 | 他们 | they (masculine or masculine and feminine) |
| 22. | tāmen | 她們 | 她们 | they (feminine only) |
| 23. | Wáng | 王 | | (a surname) |
| 24. | Huáng | 黃 | 黄 | (a surname) |
| 25. | Zhāng | 張 | 张 | (a surname) |
| 26. | Lǐ | 李 | | (a surname) |
| 27. | lǎoshī | 老師 | 老师 | teacher |
| 28. | xiānsheng | 先生 | | teacher; husband; Mr |
| 29. | tàitai | 太太 | | wife; Mrs |

# VOCABULARY

| | | | | |
|---|---|---|---|---|
| 30. xuésheng | 學生 | 学生 | | student |
| 31. shì; shi | 是 | | | to be; yes (it is so) |
| 32. bù | 不 | | | no, not (pronounced *bù* before 1st, 2nd & 3rd tone syllables; *bú* before a 4th tone syllable) |
| 33. ma | 嗎 | 吗 | | interrogative particle |

# NOTES ON GRAMMAR

## Number and Gender

Personal pronouns are made plural by adding the suffix *men*們. This suffix may also be added occasionally to nouns denoting persons to indicate plurality when it is not obvious from the context, e.g. *xuéshengmen* 學生們 but generally number is determined by context. Generally, too, there is no indication of gender in Chinese. For the third person pronoun there are three written forms according to gender (male 他, female 她, neuter 它) but they are indistinguishable in speech. The neuter *tā* 它 is not frequently used and it has no plural form.

## Names and Titles

In Chinese the order for names is surname, given name, title. Given names commonly consist of two characters and less commonly of one character. For example in the name *Wáng Xuémíng* 王學明, *Wáng* is the surname and *Xuémíng* is the given name. In the name *Zhāng lǎoshǐ* 張老師, *Zhāng* is the surname and *lǎoshǐ* means teacher (male or female). In Chinese the married woman retains her own surname except when she is addressed as *tàitai* 太太 (Mrs) e.g. *Lǐ tàitai* 李太太 means Mrs Li. In the People's Republic of China the term *àiren* 愛人 (lit: 'loved one') is widely used for husband or wife in speech; this usage does not seem to have spread to Chinese communities elsewhere.

## The Equative Sentence

In modern Chinese, sentences may be divided into several types. One is the equative sentence in which both the subject and the main part of the predicate are nouns or nominal expressions. The verb *shì* 是 equates the two and is normally pronounced in the neutral tone; if the 4th tone is used it implies emphasis.

The affirmative narrative sentence: NOMINAL EXPRESSION + *shi* + NOMINAL EXPRESSION

我是中國人。
我是老師。
你們是學生。
老師是日本人。

In the negative narrative sentence the verb *shi* is negated by the negative adverb *bù* 不 which in this case is

pronounced in the 2nd tone, i.e. *búshi*.
NOMINAL EXPRESSION + *búshi* + NOMINAL EXPRESSION

他不是中國人。
我不是老師。
張太太不是澳大利亞人。
李先生不是學生。

The interrogative sentence is formed in the following ways:
a) By placing the interrogative particle *ma* 嗎 at the end of a narrative sentence (either affirmative or negative). The negative sentence with *ma* expects an answer in the affirmative, e.g. 'Aren't you Chinese?' is *Nǐ búshi Zhōngguorén ma?*

NOMINAL EXPRESSION + *shi* + NOMINAL EXPRESSION + *ma*

你是李先生嗎？　是，我是李英生。
他是學生嗎？　是，他是學生。
張先生是老師嗎？　是，他是老師。

NOMINAL EXPRESSION + *búshi* + NOMINAL EXPRESSION + *ma*

他不是學生嗎？　不是，他是老師。
你不是老師嗎？　是，我是老師。

b) By using both the affirmative and negative forms of the verb; in this case both are pronounced in the neutral tone. The construction is called the 'alternative-type' question.
NOMINAL EXPRESSION + *shibushi* + NOMINAL EXPRESSION

你是不是英國人？　是，我是英國人。
他是不是張老師？　是，他是張老師。

NOMINAL EXPRESSION + *shi* + NOMINAL EXPRESSION + *bushi*

你是學生不是？　不是，我是老師。
他是老師不是？　是，他是老師。
她是法國人不是？　是，她是法國人。

# EXERCISES

**A.** Translate into Chinese:
1. Huang: Are you Wang Xueying?
2. Wang: Yes, I am Wang Xueying.
3. Huang: Are you a student?
4. Wang: Yes, I am a student.
5. Huang: Are you American?
6. Wang: No, I am Australian.

**B.** Translate into English:
1. 王美英：我是王美英，我是學生．
   你是學生嗎？
2. 張國本：是，我是學生。
3. 王美英：你是日本人不是？
4. 張國本：不是，我是中國人。
5. 王美英：老師是不是中國人？
6. 張國本：是，老師是中國人。

**C.** Answer in Chinese the following questions on the dialogue in B:

1. 王美英是學生嗎？
2. 老師是日本人不是？
3. 張國本是中國人嗎？

**LESSON TWO**

# VOCABULARY

| | | | |
|---|---|---|---|
| 1. líng | 零 | | zero (often represented in Chinese by zero, e.g. 101 一百〇一 ) |
| 2. yī | 一 | | one (pronounced *yī* before a pause e.g. in counting; *yì* before a 1st, 2nd, or 3rd tone syllable; *yí* before a 4th tone syllable) |
| 3. èr | 二 | | two (used in numbers and counting) |
| 4. liǎng | 兩 | 两 | two (used for specifying two items of a commodity, e.g. 'two students'; 'two houses') |
| 5. sān | 三 | | three |
| 6. sì | 四 | | four |
| 7. wǔ | 五 | | five |
| 8. liù | 六 | | six |
| 9. qī | 七 | | seven |
| 10. bā | 八 | | eight |
| 11. jiǔ | 九 | | nine |
| 12. shí | 十 | | ten |
| 13. bǎi | 百 | | hundred |
| 14. qiān | 千 | | thousand |
| 15. wàn | 萬 | 万 | ten thousand |
| 16. yǒu | 有 | | to have |
| 17. méiyǒu | 沒有 | | not to have |
| 18. zhè | 這 | 这 | this |
| 19. nà | 那 | | that |
| 20. zhèxie | 這些 | 这些 | these |
| 21. nàxie | 那些 | | those |
| 22. ge | 個 | 个 | classifier for person — polite form is *wèi* 位 ; a general classifier |
| 23. běn | 本 | | classifier for book or magazine i.e. a particular copy |
| 24. shū | 書 | 书 | book (cl. 本 ) |
| 25. zhāng | 張 | 张 | classifier for flat objects e.g. sheet, table, chair, paper |
| 26. zhǐ | 紙 | 纸 | paper (cl. 張 ) |

# VOCABULARY

| 27. fèn | 份 | 分 | classifier for particular newspapers or magazines, e.g. 'I subscribe to this magazine' |
| 28. baò(zhǐ) | 報(紙) | 报(纸) | newspaper (cl.份,張) |
| 29. zázhì | 雜誌 | 杂志 | magazine, journal (cl.本,份) |
| 30. zhǐ | 枝 | 支 | classifier for long pointed objects, e.g. pencil, branch |
| 31. bǐ | 筆 | 笔 | writing implement (cl.枝) |
| 32. máobǐ | 毛筆 | 毛笔 | writing brush (cl.枝) |
| 33. qiānbǐ | 鉛筆 | 铅笔 | pencil (cl.枝) |
| 34. yuánzhūbǐ | 圓珠筆 | 圆珠笔 | ballpoint pen (cl.枝) |
| 35. bēizi | 杯子 | | cup (cl.個) |
| 36. bēi | 杯 | | cup of, e.g. 一杯水, a cup of water |
| 37. shuǐ | 水 | | water |

# NOTES ON GRAMMAR

## Numerals

**1.** The numbers 11 to 19 are formed in the following ways:

| | |
|---|---|
| 11 *shíyī* 十一 | 16 *shíliù* 十六 |
| 12 *shí'èr* 十二 | 17 *shíqī* 十七 |
| 13 *shísān* 十三 | 18 *shíbā* 十八 |
| 14 *shísì* 十四 | 19 *shíjiǔ* 十九 |
| 15 *shíwǔ* 十五 | |

**2.** If one of the numbers 11 to 19 occurs in a larger number, *shí* is usually preceded by *yì*, e.g. 512 *wǔbǎi yìshi'èr* 五百一十二. Note that here 十 is pronounced in the neutral tone.

**3.** 20, 30, 40 etc. are formed in this way: 20 *èrshí* 二十, i.e. two tens; 30 *sānshí* 三十; 40 *sìshí* 四十 etc. Consequently, 21 *èrshiyī* 二十一; 31 *sānshiyī* 三十一; 41 *sìshiyī* 四十一 etc. Note that here 十 is pronounced in the neutral tone.

**4.** There are two words for 'two': *èr* 二, which is used as an abstract number and in compound numbers, and *liǎng* 兩. These two words differ in usage: *liǎng* is generally used before classifiers e.g. *liǎngzhī bǐ* 兩枝筆. If 'two' is part of a large number e.g. 12, 20, 22 the word *èr* is used. In the numbers 200, 2000 and 20,000 either *èr* or *liǎng* may be used.

**5.** 'Zero': *líng* 零 is used in compound numbers and in scientific language. In a large number, if an intermediate unit is '0', *líng* must be used. If the number has more than one intermediate '0' the first *líng* may be omitted. When numerals are read out as when giving telephone numbers, each '0' which appears must be read as *líng*. In such cases the character 零 is often written as '0' while it is still read as *líng*, e.g. 007 will most likely be written 〇〇七 and read *líng líng qī*.

**6.** Chinese numbers advance as follows: ten, *shí* 十; hundred, *bǎi* 百; thousand, *qiān* 千; ten thousand, *wàn* 萬; and in this system any multiple which advances the number to the next place must be called by the appropriate name, e.g. 1,900 cannot be designated 'nineteen hundred', instead *yìqiān jiǔbǎi* 一千九百 'one thousand nine hundred' must be used.

**7.** Approximate numbers are expressed in the following ways: '3 or 4 persons' is 三、四個人 and '30 or 40 books' is 三、四十本書. etc.

**8.** Examples of compound numbers (note the use of *líng*):

| | | | |
|---|---|---|---|
| 101 | 一百零一 | 1,010 | 一千零一十 |
| 109 | 一百零九 | 1,100 | 一千一(百) |
| 110 | 一百一(十) | 9,999 | 九千九百九十九 |
| 111 | 一百一十一 | 10,001 | 一萬零一 |
| 119 | 一百一十九 | 10,010 | 一萬零一十 |
| 120 | 一百二(十) | 10,100 | 一萬零一百 |
| 199 | 一百九十九 | 11,000 | 一萬一(千) |
| 1,001 | 一千零一 | 60,502 | 六萬(零)五百零二 |

# NOTES ON GRAMMAR

## Classifiers

In modern Chinese a numeral or a demonstrative adjective cannot be used directly with a noun. (There are a few exceptions to this rule e.g. *tiān* 天 meaning 'day' and *nián* 年 meaning 'year' and other such words which are themselves measure words and may be called 'quasi-classifiers'.) Generally a classifier must stand between the numeral, demonstrative adjective and certain other adjectives and the noun. Most nouns have specific classifiers or else use the general classifier *ge* 個 . However, these may be replaced by other classifiers when the context demands this. For example, 'one pencil' and 'ten pencils' would require the classifier *zhī* 枝, but 'a box of pencils' and a 'bundle of pencils' would require the words 'box' and 'bundle' respectively as classifiers. The indefinite article 'a' is *yì* 一 ('one') + classifier, e.g. 'a man' is *yíge rén* 一個人 , while the definite article 'the' is *zhè* 這 ('this') + classifier e.g. 'the man' is *zhège rén* 這個人.

**1.** When both a demonstrative adjective and numeral occur, the following pattern is used: DEMONSTRATIVE ADJECTIVE + NUMERAL + CLASSIFIER + NOUN

It should be noted that the numeral 'one' is usually omitted in this pattern. Therefore, 'this student' is *zhège xuésheng* 這個學生 while 'these two students' is *zhè liǎngge xuésheng* 這兩個學生。

**2.** When the noun is clearly defined in the context, it may be omitted; the demonstrative adjective plus the classifier are sufficient, e.g. 'These three students are Chinese, those two are Japanese' is *Zhè sānge xuésheng shi Zhōngguorén, nà liǎngge shi Rìběnrén* 這三個學生是中國人，那兩個是日本人.

**3.** When 'these' and 'those' do not refer to a specific number, *zhèxie* 這些 and *nàxie* 那些 are used. Note that the classifier is dropped. For example, 'these books' is *zhèxie shu* 這些書 and 'those magazines' is *nàxie zázhì* 那些雜誌. *Zhèxie* and *nàxie* may also be used as demonstrative pronouns, e.g. 'These are books and those are magazines' is *Zhèxie shi shū, nàxie shi zázhì* 這些是書,那些是雜誌。

**4.** When there is an adjective qualifying a noun, it stands in front of the noun after the classifier: NUMERAL + CLASSIFIER + ADJECTIVE + NOUN

'Three Chinese students' is *sānge Zhōngguó xuésheng* 三個中國學生 and 'these three Chinese students' is *zhè sānge Zhōngguó xuésheng* 這三個中國學生。

**5.** When the adjective qualifies the classifier the adjective must stand before the classifier, e.g. 'a large sheet of paper' is 一大張紙 and 'three large cups of water' is 三大杯水。

## The Sentence Using *yǒu* 有

The affirmative narrative sentence: SUBJECT + *yǒu* + OBJECT

老師有兩本書。
他有三個杯子。
我有兩杯水。
那個學生有三本書。
這些日本人有毛筆。

The negative narrative sentence: SUBJECT + *méiyǒu* + OBJECT

他們沒有那份雜誌。
這些學生沒有報紙。
這個人沒有鉛筆。
我沒有圓珠筆。
她沒有杯子。

The interrogative sentence may be formed by the use of the interrogative particle *ma* 嗎 or else the use of the 'alternative-type' question pattern.

你有毛筆嗎？　　沒有。
他們有杯子嗎？　　有，他們有三個。
你們有沒有書？　　沒有。
學生有沒有雜誌？　　他們沒有。
你有報沒有？　　我沒有。

# EXERCISES

**A.** Translate into Chinese:
1.  38; 87; 106; 115; 1,002; 1,302; 20,040; 23,104;
    20,307
2.  They do not have these two books.
3.  I have five sheets of paper.
4.  Do you have a pencil? No, I do not.
5.  This is a magazine and that is a newspaper.

**B.** Translate into English:

1.  我沒有那本書。
2.  他們有三枝筆。
3.  你們有報紙嗎？
4.  他有一萬零四張紙。
5.  我們有兩杯水。
6.  這些是鉛筆，那些是圓珠筆。
7.  我沒有這兩份雜誌。
8.  他有兩千本書。
9.  那九個學生沒有筆。
10. 這兩個學生有杯子。

**LESSON THREE**

# VOCABULARY

| | | | | |
|---|---|---|---|---|
| 1. zhǒng | 種 | 种 | | sort, type; a common classifier |
| 2. jiàn | 件 | | | item; classifier for clothing, event and thing |
| 3. dōngxi | 東西 | 东西 | | thing, object (cl.件, 個) |
| 4. fāngfa | 方法 | | | method (cl.個) |
| 5. péngyou | 朋友 | | | friend (cl.個) |
| 6. tóngxué | 同學 | 同学 | | fellow-student (cl.個) |
| 7. tài | 太 | | | too (excessive) |
| 8. hěn | 很 | | | very |
| 9. hǎo | 好 | | | good; 你好? 'How are you?', 'Hello'; … 好 不好? 'How about… ?', 'Will… be all right?' |
| 10. dà | 大 | | | big |
| 11. xiǎo | 小 | | | small |
| 12. xīn | 新 | | | new |
| 13. jiù | 舊 | 旧 | | old (for inanimate objects) |
| 14. zhòng | 重 | | | heavy |
| 15. qīng | 輕 | 轻 | | light (not heavy) |
| 16. lǎo | 老 | | | old (of people, animals) |
| 17. niánqīng | 年輕 | 年轻 | | young (of people) |
| 18. guì | 貴 | 贵 | | expensive |
| 19. piányi | 便宜 | | | cheap |
| 20. gāoxìng | 高興 | 高兴 | | happy, in high spirits |
| 21. shēngqì | 生氣 | 生气 | | angry |
| 22. …xíngbuxing | 行不行 | | | 'Will… be all right?' |
| 23. búcuò | 不錯 | 不错 | | not bad (i.e. quite good) |
| 24. diànyǐng | 電影 | 电影 | | movie (cl.個; bù 部) |
| 25. suǒ | 所 | | | classifier for house, school |
| 26. fángzi | 房子 | | | house (cl.所) |
| 27. wūzi | 屋子 | | | room (cl. jiān 間) |
| 28. xuéxiào | 學校 | 学校 | | school (cl.所, 個) |

# VOCABULARY

| 29. | dàxué | 大學 | 大学 | university (cl.所 , 個 ) |
| 30. | shāngdiàn | 商店 | | shop (cl.*jiā* 家 , 個 ) |
| 31. | túshūguǎn | 圖書館 | 图书馆 | library (cl. 個 ) |

# NOTES ON GRAMMAR

## The Sentence with an Adjectival Predicate

Chinese adjectives can function as verbs, hence in a sentence with an adjectival predicate the verb 'to be' 是 is not used. For example, 'He is happy' is *Tā hěn gāoxìng* 他很高興. In an affirmative narrative sentence of this type, the adjective is generally modified by the adverb *hěn* 很 ('very') which when used in this construction is weak in meaning. Other adverbs may replace *hěn* to modify 'is happy', e.g. 'He is extremely happy' *Tā fēicháng gāoxìng* 他非常高興 or 'This house is too old' *Zhèsuǒ fángzi tài jiù* 這所房子太舊 . An adjectival predicate without a modifier implies comparison, e.g. *Zhèsuǒ fángzi jiù* 這所房子舊 (This house is old) would also imply *Nàsuǒ fángzi xīn* 那所房子新 (That house is new).

The affirmative narrative sentence: SUBJECT + ADVERB MODIFIER + ADJECTIVE
Using the adverbial modifer *hěn* 很 :

他們很生氣。　　　這枝筆很便宜。
我們很高興。　　　那所房子很新。
這些書很貴。　　　這兩本雜誌很舊。

Using the adverbial modifier *tài* 太 (excessive):

這些東西太貴。　　這家商店太小。
他們太年輕。　　　那件東西太重。
這間屋子太大。　　那兩所房子太大。

The negative narrative sentence: SUBJECT + *bù* + ADJECTIVE

這些東西不輕。　　我不生氣。
那三件東西不重。　那個朋友不高興。
這兩間屋子不小。　這些筆不便宜。

The interrogative sentence:
SUBJECT + ADJECTIVE + *ma*

這個東西重嗎？　　不重，很輕。
這份雜誌好嗎？　　這份雜誌很好。
這家商店很大嗎？是，這家商店很大。

SUBJECT + ADJECTIVE + *bù* + ADJECTIVE
In this alternative-type interrogative sentence the words of the second part of the alternative are pronounced in the neutral tone. It should be noted that *hěn* 很 is not used in this construction, e.g. 'Is this book good?' is *Zhèběn shū hǎobuhao?* 這本書好不好?

這兩本書貴不貴？　這兩本書不貴。
那些房子新不新？　新。

# EXERCISES

**A.** Translate into Chinese:
1. Those students are not happy.
2. She is angry.
3. Is this method good?
4. This magazine is too expensive.
5. Those two students are young.
6. He is not old.
7. Is the teacher angry?
8. Are those two things heavy?

**B.** Translate into English:

1. 這枝圓珠筆便宜不便宜？　這枝圓珠筆不便宜 。
2. 這個方法好不好？　這個方法很不錯。
3. 這些太小嗎？　是，這些太小。
4. 那兩所房子貴不貴？　那兩所房子很貴。
5. 你生氣嗎？　我不生氣 。
6. 他太年輕嗎？　他不太年輕。
7. 這本書舊不舊？　這本書很舊。

14

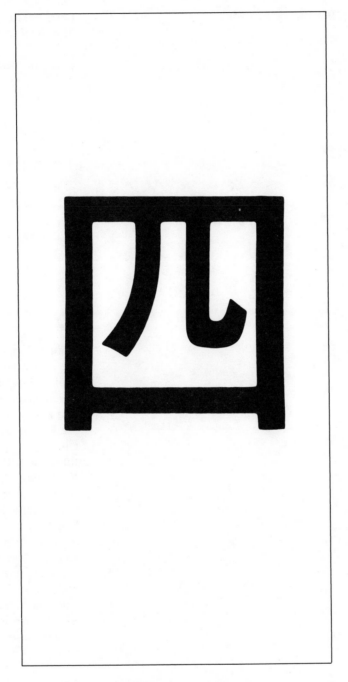

**LESSON FOUR**

# VOCABULARY

| | | | | |
|---|---|---|---|---|
| 1. | qián | 錢 | 钱 | money |
| 2. | mǐ | 米 | | rice (uncooked) |
| 3. | mǐfàn | 米飯 | 米饭 | (cooked) rice; a meal of rice as opposed to a meal of noodles, bread, etc. |
| 4. | bāo | 包 | | classifier meaning 'bag' |
| 5. | yào | 要 | | to want |
| 6. | xiǎng | 想 | | to want (aux. verb); to think |
| 7. | zhīdao | 知道 | | to know |
| 8. | xǐhuan | 喜歡 | 喜欢 | to like |
| 9. | gàosu | 告訴 | 告诉 | to tell |
| 10. | wèn | 問 | 问 | to ask |
| 11. | gěi | 給 | 给 | to give |
| 12. | xué(xi) | 學(習) | 学(习) | to study |
| 13. | Zhōngwén* | 中文 | | Chinese language [In the early stages of the movement to standardize the spoken language, a national language based on the dialect of Beijing (Peking) and known as *Guóyǔ* 國語 was promoted. This term is still used in some Chinese communities scattered throughout the world. In the People's Republic of China the term *Pǔtōnghuà* 普通話 is used when a distinction is made between the standard spoken language and dialects. What is commonly known as Chinese language is in fact the language of the Han people who constitute the largest section of the population. The terms *Hànyǔ* (spoken language of the Han people) and *Hànzì* 漢字 (written language of the Han people) are therefore favoured by academics and language teachers.] |
| 14. | Rìwén* | 日文 | | Japanese language |
| 15. | Yīngwén* | 英文 | | English language |
| 16. | Fǎwén* | 法文 | | French language |
| 17. | Éwén* | 俄文 | | Russian language |
| 18. | Éguó | 俄國 | 俄国 | Russia |
| 19. | zì | 字 | | written word |
| 20. | xiě | 寫 | 写 | to write |

# VOCABULARY

| 21. chī | 吃 | | to eat |
|---|---|---|---|
| 22. shuǐguǒ | 水果 | | fruit |
| 23. hē | 喝 | | to drink |
| 24. chá | 茶 | | tea |
| 25. kāfēi | 咖啡 | | coffee |
| 26. jiǔ | 酒 | | wine |
| 27. niúnǎi | 牛奶 | | milk (cow's milk) |
| 28. jiāo | 教 | | to teach |
| 29. kàn | 看 | | to look, to read, to watch |
| 30. tīng | 聽 | 听 | to listen |
| 31. búyào | 不要 | | do not, must not |

*When a specific reference is made to the spoken language the following terms are used: *Hànyǔ* 漢語 (Chinese), *Rìyǔ* 日語 (Japanese), *Yīngyǔ* 英語 (English), *Fǎyǔ* 法語 (French), and *Éyǔ* 俄語 (Russian).

# NOTES ON GRAMMAR

## Verb-Object Constructions

In Chinese some verbs e.g. to teach, to eat (a meal), to read, to speak and to write cannot stand alone in a sentence without an object or an implied object. If a specified object does not exist a verb-object compound is used, e.g. 'I teach' is *Wǒ jiāoshū* 我教書 whereas if the object is specified e.g. 'I teach Chinese' the verb-object compound cannot be used and instead 'Chinese' will stand as the object of the verb, i.e. *Wǒ jiāo Zhōngwén* 我教中文.

 Other examples:

'He reads' is 他看書, while 'He reads newspapers' is 他看報紙.

'He eats (a meal)' is 他吃飯, while 'He eats fruit' is 他吃水果.

'He writes' is 他寫字, while 'He writes Japanese' is 他寫日文.

'He speaks' is 他說話, while 'He speaks French' is 他說法語.

## The Simple Sentence

The grammatical construction for a simple narrative sentence in the affirmative follows the order SUBJECT + VERB (+ OBJECT):

他要兩包米。
我們學習中文。
你們學習日文。
我們告訴那個學生。
他問老師。

The negative narrative sentence: SUBJECT + NEGATIVE ADVERB + VERB ( + OBJECT)

他不要這些書。
我不喝咖啡。
他不喜歡我。
他不吃米飯。
他不知道。

The interrogative sentence: SUBJECT + VERB (+ OBJECT) + *ma*

他要錢嗎？　他不要，他要米。
你問老師嗎？　我不問，她問。
你要這些書嗎？　我要。

The alternative-type question where the second part of the alternative is pronounced in the neutral tone:
SUBJECT + VERB + NEGATIVE ADVERB + VERB (+ OBJECT)

你要不要牛奶？　不要。
他看不看報？　他不看。

SUBJECT + VERB (+ OBJECT) + NEGATIVE ADVERB + VERB

他學中文不學？　他不學中文。
你吃水果不吃？　我不吃。
你喝茶不喝？　我不喝。

# NOTES ON GRAMMAR

## Pivotal Constructions and Clause Objects

A pivotal construction consists of a VERB + NOUN + VERB sequence where the noun serves as object of the first verb and subject of the second, e.g. 'I watch the teacher writing Chinese' is *Wǒ kàn lǎoshī xiě Zhōngwén* 我看老師寫中文。

我要你教我。

我看你吃東西。

他喜歡我學中文。

他要我問老師。

張太太聽我説話。

Clause objects occur after verbs of thought or perception such as *xiǎng* (to think), *zhīdao* 知道 (to know), *shuō* 説 (to say), *tīngshuō* 聽説 (to hear that) and *wèn* 問 (to ask). In English such clauses are generally introduced by 'that' or 'whether' but in Chinese there are no equivalents for these. For example, 'He says that this writing brush is expensive' is *Tā shuō zhèzhī máobǐ hěn guì* 他説這枝毛筆很貴 and 'He asked whether the teacher wants to drink tea' is *Tā wèn lǎoshī xiǎngbuxiang hē chá* 他問老師想不想喝茶。 When *wèn* 問 (to ask) and *gàosu* 告訴 (to tell) take an indirect pronoun object which is also the subject of the following clause, the pronoun is not repeated.

## Sentences with Indirect and Direct Objects

When both an indirect object and a direct object are used, the indirect object stands first: SUBJECT + VERB + INDIRECT OBJECT + DIRECT OBJECT

他給我兩杯水。

他給我這些東西。

他給你這兩杯酒。

他教我中文。

我教你日文。

## Sentences with Auxiliary Verbs

Affirmative: SUBJECT + AUXILIARY VERB + VERB (+ OBJECT)

我想告訴他。

我想給你。

老師喜歡教中文。

我喜歡吃水果。

他要喝咖啡。

Negative: SUBJECT + NEGATIVE ADVERB + AUXILIARY VERB + VERB ( + OBJECT)

我們不想吃東西。

學生不想看雜誌。

我們不想給他。

他不喜歡聽我説話。

他們不喜歡寫字。

Interrogative:
SUBJECT + AUXILIARY VERB + VERB ( + OBJECT) + ma

你想看這本雜誌嗎?　我不想看。

你想喝這種酒嗎?　我不想喝。

你喜歡教中文嗎?　很喜歡。

你喜歡喝牛奶嗎?　不喜歡。

SUBJECT + AUXILIARY VERB + NEGATIVE ADVERB + AUXILIARY VERB + VERB ( + OBJECT)

你想不想學習日文?　不想學, 我想學法文。

你喜歡不喜歡喝酒?　喜歡喝。

你想不想吃東西?　不想吃。

# EXERCISES

**A.** Translate into Chinese:
1. Teacher likes to teach French.
2. I want to give him this cup of tea.
3. He asked me whether you were Australian.
4. They asked me whether I was Japanese.
5. He told me that you were too young.
6. She said that this pencil is not expensive.
7. They told us not to drink coffee.
8. I do not want to give her these things.

**B.** Translate into English:
1. 我不想問他。
2. 我想喝水。
3. 他很喜歡學習中文。
4. 王老師教我們法文。
5. 你喜歡不喜歡喝這種茶?
6. 他告訴我你是日本人。
7. 老師問我要不要咖啡。

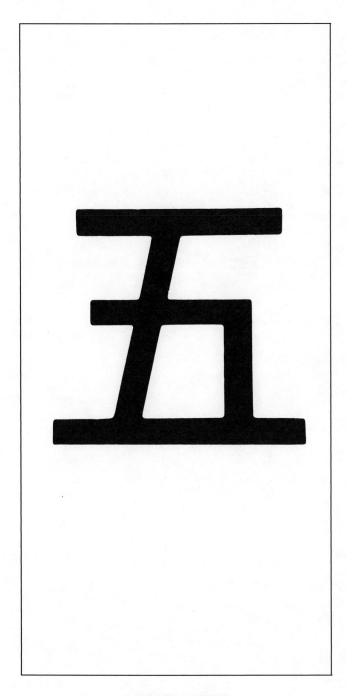

**LESSON FIVE**

# VOCABULARY

| | | | | |
|---|---|---|---|---|
| 1. zǎo | 早 | | early, 'Good morning!' |
| 2. zàijiàn | 再見 | 再见 | 'Goodbye!', 'See you again!' |
| 3. xièxie | 謝謝 | 谢谢 | 'Thank you!' |
| 4. hé | 和 | | and |
| 5. gēn | 跟 | | and |
| 6. zuò | 做 | | to do |
| 7. yòng | 用 | | to use |
| 8. tǎolùn | 討論 | 讨论 | to discuss |
| 9. shìqing | 事情 | | matter, event, happening |
| 10. wèntí | 問題 | 问题 | problem, matter, question e.g. *yǒuméiyǒu wèntí* 有没有問題? 'Are there any problems?', 'Do you have any questions?' |
| 11. dǒng | 懂 | | to understand, to comprehend |
| 12. míngbai | 明白 | | to understand, to be clear about |
| 13. gōngzuò | 工作 | | work, to work |
| 14. mǎi | 買 | 买 | to buy |
| 15. mài | 賣 | 卖 | to sell |
| 16. cháng | 長 | 长 | long |
| 17. gāo | 高 | | tall, high |
| 18. duō | 多 | | many, numerous |
| 19. shǎo | 少 | | few |
| 20. yǒuqián | 有錢 | 有钱 | rich |
| 21. yǒuyòng | 有用 | | useful |
| 22. hǎokàn | 好看 | | nice-looking |
| 23. hǎotīng | 好聽 | 好听 | fine-sounding, good to listen to |
| 24. jiǎndān | 簡單 | 简单 | simple |
| 25. zhòngyào | 重要 | | important |
| 26. tiáo | 條 | 条 | classifier for longish, winding objects e.g. snake, fish, road |
| 27. yú | 魚 | 鱼 | fish (cl. 條) |
| 28. zhōng | 鐘 | 钟 | clock (cl. 個) |

# VOCABULARY

| 29. | shǒubiǎo | 手錶 | 手表 | wristwatch (cl.*zhī* 隻; *kuài* 塊) |
|---|---|---|---|---|
| 30. | zhèyang | 這樣 | 这样 | this manner e.g. 這樣用, 'to use like this' |
| 31. | nàyang | 那樣 | 那样 | that manner e.g. 那樣做, 'to do in such a way' |
| 32. | zhèyang de | 這樣的 | 这样的 | this manner of, such e.g. 這樣的書 , 'such books' |
| 33. | nàyang de | 那樣的 | 那样的 | that manner of, such e.g. 那樣的朋友, 'such friends' |

# NOTES ON GRAMMAR

### The Connectives *gēn* 跟 and *hé* 和

The connectives *gēn* and *hé* are used interchangeably to connect substantives i.e. nouns and noun constructions but never verbal expressions or clauses. Thus 'He reads newspapers and magazines' is *Tā kàn bàozhǐ hé zázhì* 他看報紙和雜誌 while 'He reads newspapers and I read magazines' is *Tā kàn bàozhǐ, wǒ kàn zázhì* 他看報紙, 我看雜誌. In the latter case the connectives *gēn* and *hé* cannot be used.

我想買米和水果。
你和他是同學嗎?
這家商店賣水果和報紙。
你跟他是朋友嗎?
書跟雜誌很多。

### The Subordinating Particle *de* 的

**1.** Possessive case: 'My' is *wǒde* 我的 , 'your' or 'yours' is *nǐde* 你的 etc. Note however, that with nouns indicating personal relationships *de* is generally omitted after pronouns e.g. 'my wife' is *wǒ tàitai* 我太太 , 'my husband' is *wǒ xiānsheng* 我先生. The particle *de* may sometimes also be omitted after pronouns having close relationships with nouns denoting institutions and organizations e.g. 'my country', *wǒ guó* 我國 or *wǒmen guójiā* 我們國家。

我的房子太小。
這些是你的。
那些不是老師的。
我的書很少 。

**2.** The particle *de* may be used with adjectives or adjectival equivalents to express qualification. Although it is commonly used for this purpose it is not indispensable. In some cases the attributive may form an inseparable unit with its noun and *de* is not used, e.g. when the attributive is the name of a country as in 'Russian newspaper' *Éwén bào* 俄文報. Occasionally there may be a difference in meaning if *de* is used, e.g. *Zhōngguó péngyou* 中國朋友 means 'Chinese friends' while *Zhōngguó de péngyou* 中國的朋友 means 'friends of China'.

In a sentence with more than one attributive the *de* between the more closely related elements is omitted, e.g. 'This is a good student magazine' is *Zhè shi yífèn hěn hǎo de xuésheng zázhì* 這是一份很好的學生雜誌. Generally, however, the following patterns are used when nouns are qualified by adjectives:

a) When the adjective is closely knit with the noun and the resulting adjective + noun phrase can be considered the name of a category *de* is not used, e.g. *hóng bǐ* 紅筆 (red pen) as in 'Give me a red pen' where 'red pen' is a pen from the group which is red. [Cf. *hóng de bǐ* 紅的筆 which means 'a/the pen which is red' as in 'Red pens (pens which are red) are expensive'. Here *de* would grammatically introduce an attributive clause.] Many monosyllabic adjectives belong to this category, e.g.

一所大房子 (a big house)
兩個小杯子 (two small cups)
三枝新毛筆 (three new writing brushes)
十本舊雜誌 (ten old magazines)

But 'that tall student (i.e. that student who is tall)' would be 那個高的學生。
b) Reduplicated adjectives and polysyllabic adjectives must occur with *de*, e.g. *lùyóuyóu de yèzi* 綠油油的葉子 (glossy green leaves).
c) Disyllabic adjectives generally take *de*. But when the adjective modifies a literary word that has its origins in classical Chinese *de* is not used, e.g. 重要的問題 (important matters) and 重要的人 (important person) but 重要人物 (important personality).
d) When the words *duō* 多 and *shǎo* 少 are used as adjective modifiers, they must be preceded by the adverb *hěn* 很 and the particle *de* is generally not used. Thus 'few people' is *hěn shǎo rén* 很少人 and 'many people' is *hěn duō rén* 很多人 . Note that *hěn shǎo* cannot be used as an adjective modifier of the object of the verb. Hence a sentence such as 'I have few books' must be changed to 'My books are few' i.e. *wǒde shū hěn shǎo* 我的書很少 and 'He has little money' is *tāde qián hěn shǎo* 他的錢很少。

**3.** The particle *de* may be used to introduce an attributive clause. Verbs or verbal constructions take the particle *de* to form an adjectival modifier that can generally

# NOTES ON GRAMMAR

be translated into the English 'who was', 'which were', 'that were' etc. This construction follows the general rule that the qualifier precedes the word qualified. Hence the attributive clause stands before the noun and not after as it does in English.

VERB + *de* + NOUN
看的人 is 'the people who are watching'.

SUBJECT + VERB + *de* + NOUN
我用的鉛筆 is 'the pencil which I am using'.

VERB + OBJECT + *de* + NOUN
喜歡看雜誌的學生 is 'the student who likes reading magazines'.

SUBJECT + VERB + OBJECT + *de* + NOUN
你給我的東西 is 'the things which you give to me'.

**4.** The particle *de* joined to a noun, pronoun, adjective or verb forms a nominal construction meaning 'mine', 'ours', 'theirs', 'the one who' etc. Compare the sentence with an adjectival predicate and the sentence with a nominal predicate:

Adjectival predicate:
*Zhèběn shū xīnbuxīn?* 這本書新不新？
Nominal predicate:
*Zhèběn shū shi xīnde ma?* 這本書是新的嗎？
In the first case a general question is asked i.e. 'Is this book new?' while in the second case an appraisal is asked for i.e. 'Is this book a new one?' Note that in Chinese the nominal predicate sentence is very common and is often used to translate the English sentence which has an adjectival predicate. This is because sentences such as 'Is this book new?' usually imply 'Is this book a new one?'
The old one is mine. 舊的是我的。
This cup is the one he uses. 這個杯子是他用的。
He is a fish seller. 他是賣魚的.

# EXERCISES

**A.** Translate into Chinese:
1. Those cups are mine.
2. That is the house which he wants to sell.
3. The book which I want to buy is too expensive.
4. The matters which I want to discuss are few.
5. There are few students in this school.
6. He does not use a great deal of money.
7. The fruit which he sells are too small.

**B.** Translate into English:
1. 討論這些問題的人不多。
2. 買魚的人很少。
3. 他的工作不簡單。
4. 這是我買的。
5. 我想買的書太貴。
6. 這是一個很好的方法。

**C.** Translate into English:
1. 王：張先生，你好！
2. 張：王先生，你好！
3. 王：你買魚嗎？
4. 張：我想買兩條，這種魚貴不貴？
5. 王：不貴，這種魚很便宜。
6. 張：好，給我兩條。（王給張兩條魚）謝謝！
7. 王：再見！
8. 張：再見！再見！

**LESSON SIX**

# VOCABULARY

| | | | | |
|---|---|---|---|---|
| 1. | kāishǐ | 開始 | 开始 | to begin |
| 2. | zài | 在 | | (to be) in, at, on |
| 3. | shàngkè | 上課 | 上课 | to go to classes, to attend classes |
| 4. | xiàkè | 下課 | 下课 | to finish classes |
| 5. | jiàoshì | 教室 | | classroom (cl. 間) |
| 6. | diǎnzhōng | 點鐘 | 点钟 | o'clock |
| 7. | bàn | 半 | | half |
| 8. | kè (zhōng) | 刻（鐘） | 刻（钟） | quarter of an hour |
| 9. | fēn (zhōng) | 分（鐘） | 分（钟） | minute |
| 10. | xiǎoshí | 小時 | 小时 | hour (cl. 個) |
| 11. | zhōngtóu | 鐘頭 | 钟头 | hour (cl. 個) |
| 12. | chà | 差 | | almost, nearly, not up to |
| 13. | xìng | 姓 | | surname, to have the surname |
| 14. | míngzi | 名字 | | name, given name |
| 15. | jiào | 叫 | | to call, to be called (name), to tell or ask someone to do something |
| 16. | shénme | 什麼 | 什么 | what |
| 17. | nǎ | 哪 | | which |
| 18. | wèishénme | 爲什麼 | 为什么 | why, for what reason |
| 19. | yīnwei | 因爲 | 因为 | because |
| 20. | zěnme | 怎麼 | 怎么 | how, why |
| 21. | shéi, shuí | 誰 | 谁 | who |
| 22. | jǐ | 幾 | 几 | how many (less than ten) |
| 23. | duōshao | 多少 | | how many |
| 24. | suì | 歲 | 岁 | years of age |
| 25. | zhèr | 這兒 | 这儿 | here (zhèli 這裏 may also be used) |
| 26. | nàr | 那兒 | 那儿 | there (nàli 那裏 may also be used) |
| 27. | nǎr | 哪兒 | 哪儿 | where (nǎli 哪裏 may also be used) |
| 28. | dìfang | 地方 | | place |
| 29. | shíhou | 時候 | 时候 | time |

# VOCABULARY

| | | | |
|---|---|---|---|
| 30. xiànzài | 現在 | 現在 | now |
| 31. le | 了 | | modal particle indicating that a new situation has developed |

# NOTES ON GRAMMAR

## Time and Age

**1.** Time is told in the following ways — note the optional use of *guò* 過, 'past':

2.00 兩點鐘
2.10 兩點（過）十分
2.15 兩點（過）十五分；兩點（過）一刻
2.30 兩點半
2.45 兩點（過）四十五分；兩點（過）三刻；
　　　差一刻三點

a few minutes after five 五點（過）幾分
a few minutes before six 差幾分六點鐘
how many hours? 幾個小時？；幾個鐘頭？
fifteen hours 十五個小時；十五個鐘頭

**2.** Age is denoted by the addition of *suì* 歲 to a numerical unit e.g. ten years of age 十歲。

**3.** Enquiries about time and age often make use of the modal particle *le* 了 to indicate that a new situation has arisen:
What is his age? 他幾歲了？
What is the time? 幾點鐘了？

**4.** Responses to enquiries about time and age also make use of the modal particle *le* 了.
It is four o'clock (it has become four o'clock).
四點鐘了。
He is ten years of age (he has become ten years of age).
他十歲了。

## Interrogative Pronouns, Adjectives and Adverbs

Interrogative sentences may be formed by using interrogative pronouns, adjectives or adverbs. In such sentences no further indication of the interrogative is necessary. The interrogative particle *ma* 嗎 is not used at the end of the sentence. The word order in these sentences remains unchanged and the position of the interrogative pronoun, adjective or adverb is determined by whether it is the subject, verb, complement or object of the sentence. Hence *Zhè shi yìběn shū* 這是一本書 'This is a book' could be the answer to the question *Zhè shi shénme* 這是什麼 'What is this?' (This is what) and the sentence *Zhè shi Éwén bào* 這是俄文報 'This is a Russian newspaper' could be the answer to the question *Zhè shi shénme bào* 這是什麼報 'What (kind of) newspaper is this?'

**1.** *Shénme* 什麼

a) as an interrogative pronoun:
這是什麼？　　這是毛筆。
那些是什麼？　　那些是雜誌。
他姓什麼？　　他姓王。
他想做什麼？　　他想吃東西。

b) as an interrogative adjective:
這是什麼東西？　　這是毛筆。
你叫什麼名字？　　我叫文英。
你做什麼工作？　　我教書。
你想吃什麼東西？　　我想吃水果。
你上什麼課？　　我上中文課。

**2.** *Jǐ* 幾 is an interrogative adjective used for numbers under 10:
你要幾枝毛筆？　　五枝。
幾點鐘了？　　八點一刻。
他有幾本書？　　三本。
你要買幾條魚？　　兩條。
你要買幾包米？　　三包。

**3.** *Duōshao* 多少 may be used as an interrogative adjective or pronoun and may refer to any number:
你要多少錢？　我要很多。
你懂多少法文？　　很少。
你要多少？　　三十個。
你要多少本書？　　五本。
你要多少枝筆？　　九枝。

**4.** *Nǎ* 哪 — interrogative adjective:
你是哪國人？　　我是法國人。
他是哪國人？　　日本人。
你要哪本書？　　這本。
你要哪些東西？　　這些。
哪所學校好？　　這所。

**5.** *Nǎr* 哪兒 — interrogative pronoun:
他在哪兒？　　他在學校。
他在哪兒？　　他在日本。
老師在哪兒？　　他在圖書館。
你的新房子在哪兒？
圖書館在哪兒？

# NOTES ON GRAMMAR

**6.** *Wèishénme* 為什麼 — interrogative adverb:

他為什麼不給你? 因為他很生氣。
你為什麼不要這本書? 因為太舊。
你為什麼不買房子? 因為我沒有錢。

**7.** *Zěnme* 怎麼 may be used as an interrogative adverb meaning 'how':

這個字怎麼寫?
那個東西怎麼用?
這樣的東西怎麼吃?

**8.** *Zěnme* 怎麼 can also function as an interrogative adverb asking 'how is it that' or 'why' while at the same time denoting surprise that the action has taken place:

他怎麼不知道?
你怎麼不告訴他?
他怎麼不吃?

**9.** *Zěnmeyàng* 怎麼樣 can function as an interrogative pronoun meaning 'what kind':

他的新房子怎麼樣? 他的新房子很好。
那個學生怎麼樣? 他是一個很好的學生。

**10.** *Shéi/shuí* 誰 is an interrogative pronoun:

他是誰? 他是我的老師。
這是誰的毛筆? 是王先生的。

**Attributive Clauses formed with *shíhou* 時候 and *dìfang* 地方**

... 的時候 is used to translate 'when', 'at the time when':

上課的時候,不要吃東西。
老師說話的時候,不要看書。

... 的地方 is used to translate 'where', 'the place where':

你工作的地方在哪兒?
這是我上課的地方。

# EXERCISES

**A.** Translate into Chinese:
1.  How old is she? She is eleven years old.
2.  What time is it? It is half past six.
3.  Where is he? He is in Japan.
4.  Whose chair is this? It is his.
5.  What is his surname? His surname is Huang.
6.  What does your friend want? I do not know.

**B.** Translate into English:

1. 老師:你叫什麼名字?
2. 學生:我是王文英,我想學中文。
3. 老師:王文英,你幾歲了?
4. 學生:我十歲了。
5. 老師:你有沒有毛筆?
6. 學生:有,我有三枝。一枝新的,兩枝舊的。

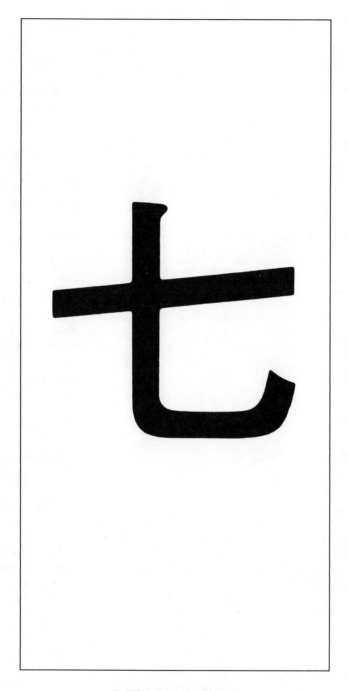

**LESSON SEVEN**

# VOCABULARY

| | | | | |
|---|---|---|---|---|
| 1. | xiǎo háir | 小孩兒 | | child, children; the words *háir* 孩兒, *xiǎo háizi* 小孩子 and *háizi* 孩子 are also commonly used |
| 2. | qù | 去 | | to go |
| 3. | lái | 來 | 来 | to come |
| 4. | shàng | 上 | | to ascend: *shàngqu* 上去 to go up; *shànglai* 上來 to come up |
| 5. | xià | 下 | | to descend: *xiàqu* 下去 to go down; *xiàlai* 下來 to come down |
| 6. | huí | 回 | | to return: *huíqu* 回去 to go back; *huílai* 回來 to come back |
| 7. | jiā | 家 | | home |
| 8. | jiāli | 家裏 | 家里 | home |
| 9. | huíjiā | 回家 | | to return home |
| 10. | chū | 出 | | to exit: *chūqu* 出去 to go out; *chūlai* 出來 to come out |
| 11. | jìn | 進 | 进 | to enter: *jìnqu* 進去 to go in; *jìnlai* 進來 to come in, 'Come in!' |
| 12. | qǐlai | 起來 | 起来 | to get up |
| 13. | guo | 過 | 过 | verbal suffix indicating that an action took place in the past |
| 14. | guò | 過 | 过 | to go past, to go over: *guòqu* 過去 to go over; *guòlai* 過來 to come over |
| 15. | ná | 拿 | | to take in the hand(s): *náqu* 拿去 to take away; *nálai* 拿來 to bring; *náchuqu* 拿出去 to take outside; *náchulai* 拿出來 to take out of; *náqilai* 拿起來 to pick up |
| 16. | zhàn | 站 | | to stand: *zhànqilai* 站起來 to stand up |
| 17. | zuò | 坐 | | to sit: *zuòxialai* 坐下來 to sit down |
| 18. | zǒu | 走 | | to walk, to depart: *zǒuguoqu* 走過去 to go over, *zǒuguolai* 走過來 to come over; *zǒulù* 走路 to walk (as opposed to running or moving from one place to another by some other means) |
| 19. | kū | 哭 | | to weep: *kūchulai* 哭出來 to burst into tears |
| 20. | xiào | 笑 | | to laugh, smile: *xiàochulai* 笑出來 to burst into laughter |
| 21. | pǎo | 跑 | | to run |

# VOCABULARY

| 22. biàn | 遍 | | time(s) i.e. to go through the process of doing something, e.g. *yíbiàn* 一遍, *liǎngbiàn* 兩遍 (once, twice) |
| 23. cì | 次 | | time(s) i.e. occurrence of an action, e.g. *yícì* 一次, *liǎngcì* 兩次 (once, twice) |
| 24. jīntian | 今天 | | today |
| 25. jīnnián | 今年 | | this year |
| 26. yánse | 顏色 | 颜色 | colour |
| 27. huáng(se) | 黃(色) | 黄(色) | yellow |
| 28. hóng(se) | 紅(色) | 红(色) | red |
| 29. hēi(se) | 黑(色) | | black |
| 30. bái(se) | 白(色) | | white |
| 31. qǐng | 請 | 请 | please, to invite |

# NOTES ON GRAMMAR

## Please

In short commands, *qǐng* 請 is used alone, e.g. *qǐng jìn* 請進 'please come in!'; *qǐng zuò* 請坐, 'please be seated' or 'please take a seat'. However, in longer sentences *qǐng* is usually followed by *nǐ* 你 or *nǐmen* 你們. *Qǐng* of course may be used as a full verb meaning 'to invite' e.g. *Wǒ xiǎng qǐng lǎoshī chīfàn* 我想請老師吃飯 'I want to invite the teacher to (eat) a meal'.

Please tell me his name. 請你告訴我他的名字。

Please start writing. 請你開始寫字。

Please give me three sheets of paper. 請你給我三張紙。

## Colours

'What colour is this?': When the implied meaning is 'What is the colour of this?' it is *Zhè shi shénme yánse de* 這是什麼顏色的 whereas if the implied meaning is 'What is this colour?', it is *Zhè shi shénme yánse* 這是什麼顏色? Similarly, 'This is red' i.e. 'This is red in colour' is *Zhè shi hóngse de* 這是紅色的 whereas if the implied meaning is 'This is the colour red' it is *Zhè shi hóngse* 這是紅色.

What is the colour of this? 這是什麼顏色的?

What is the colour of this thing? 這個東西是什麼顏色的?

What is the colour of this sheet of paper? 這張紙是什麼顏色的?

This sheet of paper is white. 這張紙是白色的。

What is this colour? 這是什麼顏色?
This is (the colour) red. 這是紅色。
This is (the colour) black. 這是黑色。
What colour are these? 這些是什麼顏色的?
These are red. 這些是紅色的。

## Directional Complements

**1.** The simple directional complement: The verbs *lái* 來 and *qù* 去 are often used after another verb as a complement which shows the direction of the action. If the action is towards the speaker, 來 is used and if the action is away from the speaker, 去 is used, e.g. *qǐng jìnlai* 請進來 would be said by someone in a room in answer to a knock on the door, while *qǐng jìnqu* 請進去 would be said by someone outside a room inviting another person to go in. Note that the complement is pronounced in the neutral tone.

我們上去。
他不想下去。
他今天回來。
他們進去。
小孩兒想進來。

**2.** The compound directional complement: Verbs of motion can take 來 and 去 to form compound directional complements. In these cases the first element shows the direction of movement e.g. *shàng* 上 'up', *xià* 下 'down', *jìn* 進 'in', *chū* 出 'out', *huí* 回 'back' and the second

# NOTES ON GRAMMAR

element shows the direction of the action with regard to the speaker. Thus the complement *shàngqu* 上去 means 'up' (away from the speaker) while *shànglai* 上來 means 'up' (towards the speaker). Both elements of the complement are pronounced in the neutral tone.

Towards the speaker:

小孩兒跑過來。

他們走進來。

Away from the speaker:

他跑下去。

他們走出去。

**3.** The directional complement with an object:

a) The object of a verb with a simple directional complement is placed between the verb and the complement.

小孩兒想回家去。

學生回學校來。

他們走進房子去。

我們拿酒去。

b) The object of a verb with a compound directional complement usually is inserted between the two elements which make up the directional complement. This pattern is imperative when the object is a noun indicating locality.

學生跑進教室來。

小孩兒走進房子去。

他拿出什麼東西來？

小孩兒拿出一枝毛筆來。

However, if the action of the verb causes the position of the object to change, the object may be placed after the complement.

他拿出來三枝圓珠筆。

他拿出來兩個杯子。

他拿出去三枝鉛筆。

他拿過來這包水果。

他拿過來兩個杯子。

## The Verbal Suffix *guo* 過 Indicating Past Experience

*Guo* is used to indicate that an action or event did or did not occur in the past. The negative is formed by placing *méi* 沒 or *méiyou* 没有 before the VERB + *guo* sequence. *Guo* may be used to indicate that the action or event occurred or did not occur at a specific time in the past or at least once in the indefinite past. Note that when *guo* is used for a precise moment of time, it occurs only in the affirmative, e.g. 'He came at eight o'clock' (where the implication is that he is no longer there) is *Tā bā diǎnzhōng láiguo* 他八點鐘來過 whereas 'He did not come at eight o'clock' is *Tā bā diǎnzhōng méiyou lái* 他八點鐘没有來. In the latter, *méiyou* is the negative of the suffix *le* (see Lesson Nine) for if he did not come at eight o'clock he still has not come; his coming is thus not an event of the past and *guo* cannot be used.

Affirmative pattern:

他今年來過。

他今年來過兩次。

Negative pattern:

他今年没來過。

我没看過那本書。

Interrogative patterns:

a) 他今年來過嗎？　　來過，他來過三次。

你看過這本書嗎？　　看過，我看過兩遍。

你用過這個新方法嗎？　　没用過。

b) 他今天來過没有？　　來過，他八點來過。

你看過他没有？　　看過。

你喝過這種茶没有？　　喝過一次。

c) 這兩份雜誌，你看過没有？　　我看過。

那種東西，你吃過没有？　　没吃過。

這種新酒，你喝過没有？　　喝過。

---

# EXERCISES

**A.** Translate into Chinese:
1. What colour is your cup?
2. Why does he want to go up?
3. Why does he not want to come out?
4. They run into the house.
5. He takes out (of something) a magazine.
6. Have you used it?
7. Yes, I have used it twice.

**B.** Translate into English:
1. 那個名字，我聽過很多次。
2. 他的舊房子是什麼顏色的？
3. 他今天來過兩次。
4. 這三包水果是誰拿來的？
5. 學生為什麼跑進教室去？

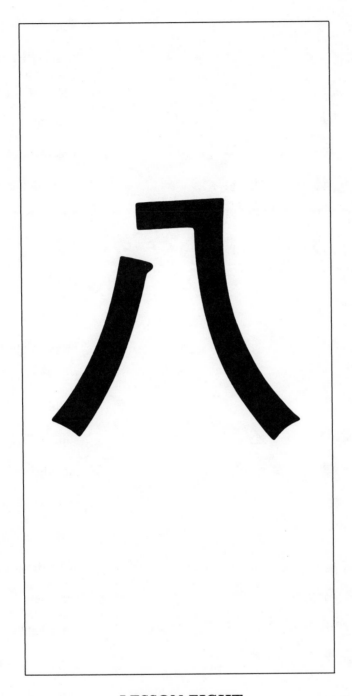

**LESSON EIGHT**

# VOCABULARY

| | | | | |
|---|---|---|---|---|
| 1. wán(r) | 玩(兒) | 玩(儿) | | to play, to enjoy oneself |
| 2. shǒu | 首 | | | classifier for song or poem |
| 3. gē | 歌 | | | song (cl. 首 ) |
| 4. chàng | 唱 | | | to sing; 'He sings' *Tā chànggē* 他唱歌 |
| 5. yìqǐ | 一起 | | | together |
| 6. yíkuàir | 一塊兒 | 一块儿 | | together |
| 7. yígòng | 一共 | | | together |
| 8. kuài (qián) | 塊(錢) | 块(钱) | | *yuan*, dollar |
| 9. máo (qián) | 毛(錢) | 毛(钱) | | 10 cents |
| 10. fēn (qián) | 分(錢) | 分(钱) | | 1 cent |
| 11. yě | 也 | | | also |
| 12. dōu | 都 | | | all |
| 13. yòu | 又 | | | again, also, furthermore |
| 14. xiān | 先 | | | first |
| 15. zài | 再 | | | again |
| 16. hái | 還 | 还 | | still, still more |
| 17. yǐjǐng | 已經 | 已经 | | already |
| 18. yídìng | 一定 | | | certainly |
| 19. zhǐ | 只 | | | only |
| 20. chángcháng | 常常 | | | often, frequently |
| 21. fēicháng | 非常 | | | extremely |
| 22. lìkè | 立刻 | | | immediately |
| 23. gāngcái | 剛才 | 刚才 | | just (short time ago) |
| 24. de | 得 | | | structural particle indicating adverb of manner |
| 25. de | 地 | | | adverbial suffix |
| 26. kuài | 快 | | | fast |
| 27. màn | 慢 | | | slow |
| 28. lǎoshi | 老實 | 老实 | | honest |
| 29. qīngchu | 清楚 | | | clear |

# VOCABULARY

| 30. míngbai | 明白 | | clear |
| 31. máng | 忙 | | busy |
| 32. hòulái | 後來 | 后来 | afterwards |

# NOTES ON GRAMMAR

## Monetary Expressions

**1.** Documents such as contracts, receipts, cheques and price tags use the terms *yuán* 元 (dollar) and *jiǎo* 角 (ten cents). Hence 10.55 yuan is 十元五角五分 and 2.25 yuan is 二元二角五分。

**2.** The spoken form and other written forms use the terms *kuài* 塊, *máo* 毛 and *fēn* 分 in the following ways:

1.00 *yuan* is 一塊錢
0.50 *yuan* is 五毛錢
0.05 *yuan* is 五分錢
2.00 *yuan* is 兩塊錢
2.25 *yuan* is 兩塊兩毛五分錢
2.02 *yuan* is 兩塊零兩分
How much does this book cost? 這本書多少錢？
How much does this pencil cost? 這枝鉛筆多少錢？
How much do these two books cost? 這兩本書多少錢？
This house costs $50,000. 這所房子五萬塊錢。

## Reduplication of Adjectives

Some adjectives may be reduplicated to emphasize the quality of the adjective; this reduplicated form may be used as an adverbial modifier. In such cases the adverbial suffix *de* 地 is used to join it with the verb it modifies. Note the tone changes in the elements of a reduplicated adjective:

**1.** When a monosyllabic adjective is reduplicated the second syllable is pronounced in the first tone and followed by the noun suffix *er* 兒. The noun suffix *er* however, is not usually represented in written material.
*hǎo* 好 becomes *hǎohāor* 好好兒
*kuài* 快 becomes *kuàikuāir* 快快兒
*màn* 慢 becomes *mànmānr* 慢慢兒

**2.** When a disyllabic adjective is reduplicated, the first and last syllables are stressed and the middle two syllables are pronounced in the neutral tone:
*lǎoshi* 老實 becomes *lǎolaoshishí* 老老實實
*míngbai* 明白 becomes *míngmingbaibái* 明明白白
*gāoxìng* 高興 becomes *gāogaoxingxìng* 高高興興
*qīngchu* 清楚 becomes *qīngqingchuchǔ* 清清楚楚

## Adverbial Modifiers

The normal sentence order is that the qualifier must precede the word it qualifies. Hence the position of the adverb is before the verb or its negative. The following are some common adverbs which are used under specific circumstances:

**1.** *hái* 還 'still (up to this time)' or 'still (more)'; 'yet'; 'also'; 'in addition' (for additional action by the same actor; refers to the predicate); 'more' and 'further'.
Does he still like to sing? 他還喜歡唱歌嗎？
I want another cup of coffee. 我還要一杯咖啡。
He still wants to read that book. 他還想看那本書。
He is still in China. 他還在中國。
Hasn't he told you yet? 他還沒告訴你嗎？

**2.** *yòu* 又 and *zài* 再 meaning 'again' in the sense of repetition or continuation of action. Both of these adverbs may be used to indicate repetition or continuation of action. However, *yòu* refers to events in the past while *zài* refers to events in the future. Compare the following sentences:

He came (once) at two o'clock and again at three o'clock; he said that he would come again at four or five o'clock. 他兩點鐘來過一次，三點又來過一次；他說四五點再來。

He came at five o'clock, since then he has not come again. (The action of coming has not been repeated.) 他五點鐘來過，後來沒有再來。

He asked me to repeat my name. 他叫我再說一遍我的名字。

Note that *zài* differs from other adverbial modifiers in that it may be placed after the negative adverb as well as before it. *Yòu* may be used to indicate repetition of an action in the present or future but only in cases where the action recurs periodically or is anticipated. Such sentences are usually completed with the modal particle *le* 了 to indicate the new situation which has arisen, e.g. 'He's crying again!' 他又哭了 and 'He wants to eat again!' 他又想吃了。

**3.** *yě* 也 'also' (referring to the subject), 'as well' and 'even'. The adverb *yě* indicates something additional but has no implications of time or duration, e.g. 'I am also going' 我也去 and 'He wants to go to China as well as to Japan' 他也想去中國，也想去日本. In sentences of this type the verb must be repeated in Chinese. When *yě* is used to give the meaning of 'even' the object of the sentence is placed before the verb or subject for emphasis, e.g. 'He even understands Chinese' 他中文也懂。

**4.** *zhǐ* 只 'only', indicates limitation, e.g. 'I only want one dollar' 我只要一塊錢。

**5.** *dōu* 都 'all'. As in the case of all adverbs, *dōu* must precede the verb. It is used in sentences with a plural subject and its effect is to totalize the noun or nouns before it. When *yě* 也 and *dōu* appear in the same sentence *yě* always precedes *dōu*.

We (all of us) also like reading newspapers. 我們也都喜歡看報。

Both the teacher and the students are happy. 老師和學生都高興。

These three types of houses are all ugly. 這三種房子都不好看。

## The Adverbial Suffix *de* 地

Adjectives of more than one syllable or adjectives modified by an adverb (e.g. *hěn* 很 or *bù* 不) may function as adverbial modifiers when followed by the suffix *de* 地. Adverbial modifiers with *de* are usually used in narrative sentences; they describe the manner in which the subject carries out the action. Such sentences are not restricted by time. Compare this to the usage of the complement of degree which is restricted by time and which is descriptive rather than narrative. (See below.)

ADJECTIVE + *de*
They angrily sat down. 他們生氣地坐下來了。
The students happily walk into the classroom. 學生高興地走進教室來。
They cheerfully discuss the problem. 他們高高興興地討論問題。
We like to drink tea slowly. 我們喜歡慢慢地喝茶。

ADVERB + ADJECTIVE + *de*
He very quickly tells me. 他很快地告訴我。
She unhappily walks out. 她不高興地走出去。
He very slowly picks up the book. 他非常慢地拿起書來。

## The Complement of Degree Formed with *de* 得

**1.** VERB + *de* + COMPLEMENT is a pattern used to comment on the way an action is performed, i.e. the extent or quality attained, e.g. 'How is he doing it?' or 'How did he do it?' is 他做得怎麼樣? and 'He is doing it well' or 'He did it well' is 他做得好. This construction represents a comment or judgement on an action and hence refers to an action already completed or the way an action is normally performed. If the speaker has not established what it is he wishes to comment upon he will do so before presenting his comment, e.g. 'He sings that song well' will follow the pattern SUBJECT + VERB + OBJECT + VERB + *de* + COMPLEMENT 他(唱)那首歌唱得好 or the pattern TOPIC (i.e. OBJECT) + SUBJECT + VERB + *de* + COMPLEMENT 那首歌,他唱得好。

Affirmative:
a) Where the action to be commented upon is already established.
He sings well./He sang well. 他唱得好。
He writes fast./He wrote quickly. 他寫得快。
She writes too slowly./She wrote too slowly. 她寫得太慢。
b) Where the action to be commented upon has not been established.
He writes slowly. 他寫字寫得慢。
I read slowly. 我看書看得慢。
I eat a great deal of fruit. 我吃水果吃得很多。

Negative:
他喝牛奶喝得不多。
我吃東西吃得不少。
我唱歌唱得不好。

Interrogative:
他寫字寫得好嗎?
他看書看得快嗎?
他買東西買得多嗎?
他看中文看得快不快?
他吃東西吃得多不多?

**2.** The complement of degree is often used in sentences which would take a passive verb in English.
That song was sung well. 那首歌唱得好。
His work was done extremely well. 他的工作做得非常好。
Those things were purchased very cheaply. 那些東西買得很便宜。

# EXERCISES

**A.** Translate into Chinese:
1. How much does this book cost?
2. Thirty-two dollars and fifty-five cents.
3. You are selling it extremely cheaply.
4. He likes to eat things slowly.
5. That student sings well.
6. We are all students.
7. I also want to buy a writing brush.
8. He does not want to go up again.
9. That book is selling cheaply.
10. He immediately sits down.
11. I already have a cup.
12. They told me frankly that they only wanted money.
13. Are you busy?
14. He will certainly come.
15. They are still in China.

**B.** Translate into English:
1. 他們想一起回家。
2. 我常常看中文書。
3. 我今天不忙。
4. 你先告訴老師。
5. 他已經有房子了。
6. 他一定有兩塊錢。
7. 你還想喝嗎？
8. 後來他很生氣。
9. 小孩兒剛才很高興。
10. 他們都玩得很好。
11. 我不想再告訴你。
12. 他常常哭，現在又哭了。

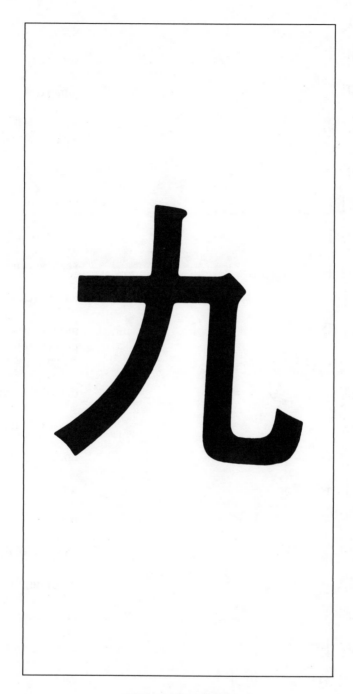

**LESSON NINE**

# VOCABULARY

| | | | |
|---|---|---|---|
| 1. le | 了 | | verbal suffix; modal particle |
| 2. jiù | 就 | | sequence indicator; then |
| 3. tiān | 天 | | day |
| 4. zuótian | 昨天 | | yesterday |
| 5. míngtian | 明天 | | tomorrow |
| 6. xīngqī | 星期 | | week (cl. 個 ); used interchangeably with *lǐbài* 禮拜 |
| 7. nián | 年 | | year |
| 8. míngnián | 明年 | | next year |
| 9. qùnián | 去年 | | last year |
| 10. qiánnián | 前年 | | year before last |
| 11. yuè | 月 | | month (cl. 個 ) |
| 12. yuèfèn | 月份 | | month (when reference is made to a particular month, e.g. 'He will come in August' 他八月份來 .) |
| 13. hào | 號 | 号 | day of the month |
| 14. rì | 日 | | day (used in dates) |
| 15. zhōngwǔ | 中午 | | noon |
| 16. shàngwǔ | 上午 | | a.m. |
| 17. xiàwǔ | 下午 | | p.m. |
| 18. zǎo | 早 | | early, 'Good morning!' |
| 19. zǎoshang | 早上 | | morning, in the morning |
| 20. wǎn | 晚 | | late, evening |
| 21. wǎnshang | 晚上 | | evening, in the evening |
| 22. jìnlái | 近來 | 近来 | recently |
| 23. kànjian | 看見 | 看见 | to see |
| 24. tīngjian | 聽見 | 听见 | to hear |
| 25. yǒu | 有 | | there is, there are (indicates existence) |
| 26. yǒude | 有的 | | some (i.e. some of) |
| 27. yǒuxie | 有些 | | some (i.e. some of) |
| 28. yìxiē | 一些 | | some, a few |
| 29. yìdiǎnr | 一點兒 | 一点儿 | some, a little (i.e. a small portion ). In the spoken language *yìdiǎnr* is often shortened to *diǎnr* |

# NOTES ON GRAMMAR

## *yǒu* 有 **Indicating Existence**

'There are' and 'there is' are usually translated by the verb *yǒu*:

There is a good library here. 這兒有一個好圖書館 。

There are three shops there. 那兒有三家商店.

There are no houses here. 這兒沒有房子 .

Is there a school there? 那兒有學校嗎?

There are no books in that place. 那個地方沒有書 .

Are there any problems? 有沒有問題 ?

## *yǒuxie* 有些 **and** *yǒude* 有的

Because *yǒu* 有 implies existence, both *yǒuxie* and *yǒude* refer to specific but unidentified persons or things and not to indefinite quantity. *Yǒuxie* and *yǒude* both have the basic meaning of 'some of' and therefore cannot be used as objects of verbs. For example, neither can be used to translate 'some' in the sentence 'I want some'. In this case *yìxie* or *yìdiǎnr* (see below) would be used. *Yǒuxie* and *yǒude* are interchangeable.

Some students do not like this method. 有的學生不喜歡這個方法 。

Some of them sing well. 有些唱得好 。

## *yìxie* 一些 **and** *yìdiǎnr* 一點兒

These terms are used when referring to indefinite quantity. *Yìdiǎnr* means 'a small portion of' or 'a bit of' and cannot be used to translate 'some' when it means 'a few'. When 'some' means 'a few' *yìxie* is used.

I still want some. 我還要一些 。

Give me some water. 給我一點兒水 。

I only want to give him some old things. 我只想給他一些舊東西 。

I want to sell some of them. 我想賣一些 。

## Time Words and Phrases

A time word or phrase, being adverbial, always precedes the verb it modifies. It may precede the subject of the sentence if it is emphasized more than the subject. The general principle is that more important or larger units precede less important or smaller units, e.g. in names the order is surname + given name, and in addresses the order is country + city + street + number. Hence in time phrases such as 'today at five o'clock in the afternoon' the order is today + afternoon + five o'clock, and 'this evening' is today + evening.

He will come tomorrow evening. 他明天晚上來.

We shall go this evening at 6 o'clock. 我們今天晚上六點鐘去 。

They came early today. 他們今天來得早.

## Days of the Week

| | | | |
|---|---|---|---|
| Monday | 星期一 | Friday | 星期五 |
| Tuesday | 星期二 | Saturday | 星期六 |
| Wednesday | 星期三 | Sunday | 星期天 ; 星期日 |
| Thursday | 星期四 | | |

What day of the week is it? 今天是星期幾 ?

Today is Monday. 今天是星期一 。

How many days are there in a week? 一個星期有幾天 ?

It's Wednesday again. 今天又是星期三了 。

last week 上個星期; next week 下個星期

## Months of the Year

| | | | |
|---|---|---|---|
| January | 一月 | February | 二月 |
| March | 三月 | April | 四月 |
| May | 五月 | June | 六月 |
| July | 七月 | August | 八月 |
| September | 九月 | October | 十月 |
| November | 十一月 | December | 十二月 |

How many months in one year? 一年有幾個月?

How many days are there in September? 九月有多少天 ?

In which month will he come? 他幾月份來 ?

He will come in October next year. 他明年十月份來 。

What day of September is it? 今天是九月幾號?

last month 上個月; next month 下個月

## Dates

What is the date today? 今天是幾號?

3rd January, 1980. 一九八〇年一月三日 。

In 1920 I was in France. 一九二〇年我在法國 。

## Tonal Changes of *yī* 一

Generally the tone of *yī* is determined by the tone of the syllable which follows it. If followed by a 4th tone syllable or a neutral tone syllable with an original 4th tone, *yī* is pronounced in the 2nd tone, e.g *yíge rén* 一個人 , *yícì* 一次. If followed by any other tone, *yī* is pronounced in the 4th tone, e.g. *yìtiáo yú* 一條魚. However, in counting and in listing numbers and when used as an ordinal number (e.g. in days of the week, months and dates) the 1st tone is used, e.g. January *yīyuè*; November *shíyīyuè*; Monday *xīngqīyī*; 1971 *yījiǔqīyīnián*.

## The Modal Particle *le* 了

A modal particle is used to indicate the mood of the clause or sentence at the end of which it stands. Modal particles are pronounced in the neutral tone. The modal particle *le* has a distinctly separate function from the verbal suffix *le*. Whereas the function of the verbal suffix *le* is used to emphasize completed action, the modal particle *le* is used to indicate that a new state or situation has emerged.

**1.** When the modal *le* is used to refer to a new state or situation in present or future action it may assume the following meanings:

a) A new action which has started and is continuing, e.g. 'He is crying' is *Tā kū le* 他哭了. This sentence may imply that he was not crying before or that the speaker has just noticed that he is crying although he may have been crying for some time. The same implications may also occur in sections b, c, d, & e.

He is no longer crying. 他不哭了。
He wants money again. 他又要錢了。
I do not want to look at it any longer. 我不想再看了。

b) Clauses and sentences with predicates indicating age or time (o'clock) generally make use of the modal particle *le*. With time expressions the modal *le* indicates 'that it has become …o'clock'. With age expressions the modal *le* indicates that a person has become 'as old as …years of age'. (See Lesson Six)

c) A mild command in response to a new situation:
Let's eat! (i.e. it has now become time to eat) 吃飯了。
Don't cry! (i.e. it has now become time to stop crying) 不要哭了。

d) Modal *le* used with adverbs such as 'soon' e.g. *yào* 要, *jiù(yào)* 就 (要) and *kuài(yào)* 快(要) implies immediate or future imminent action whereby a new state or situation will emerge:
He is about to cry. 他要哭了。
He will be going shortly. 他快要去了。
I shall be going home soon. 我就要回家了。

e) Used with adjectival predicates the modal *le* may be translated as 'is', 'am', 'are', 'has now become' etc. In some circumstances the sense 'has now become' implies excessive degree, although generally the adverb *tài* 太 (excessively) will precede the adjective, e.g. 太大了 (too big).
It has become big/It has grown big. 大了。
He is old (i.e. He has become old)/He is too old/He has grown old. 他老了。

**2.** Modal *le* may be used to emphasize that an isolated event occurred in the past, e.g.
He bought a house last year. 他去年買房子了。
I went shopping this morning. 今天早上我去買東西了。

However, modal *le* is not used in sentences describing something which happened many times in the past or which is a constant state, e.g.
Last year he often came to eat. 去年他常常來吃飯。
In 1980 he was studying Japanese in Japan. 一九八〇年他在日本學習日文。

**3.** The modal *le* may be used to emphasize action completed as of the present moment.
a) With quantified objects the verb suffix *le* is used to emphasize that the action has been completed to the specified amount and the modal *le* is used to indicate that up to the present so much of the action has been completed but that there will be future continuation of the action.
I read half of it 我看了一半。(suffix *le*)
I have read half of it (I shall read the rest later). 我看了一半了。(Here both the verb suffix *le* and the modal *le* are used.)

b) Where there is no object or where there is no implied or stated specification of the object (see below) the suffix *le* is usually absorbed by the modal *le* indicating action completed as of the present.
He has gone home. 他回家了。
They have gone back. 他們回去了。
She has gone up. 她上去了。

## The Verbal Suffix *le* 了

The verbal suffix *le* 了 is only used when one wishes to emphasize the completion of an action. It is used for events that are specific, quantified, have an inherently perfective meaning (e.g. *sǐle* 死了 'is dead, died'; *wàngle* 忘了 'forget, has forgotten') or if there are following events (e.g. *Wǒ mǎile dōngxi jiù huíjiā le* 我買了東西就回家了 'I went home after doing the shopping'). It is not used to indicate past tense, e.g. in the sentence 'In 1936 I taught in China' 一九三六年我在中國教書 the completion of the act of teaching is not emphasized, therefore the suffix *le* is not used. The suffix *le* can also be used to indicate completion of an action in the future, e.g. 'My wife will come next year after I have bought a house' 明年我買了房子我太太就來。

**1.** SUBJECT + VERB + SUFFIX *le* + SPECIFIED OBJECT

In verb + object sentences where completion of the action is emphasized the object is usually specified in some way. Even if the object is not specified in English it would usually be specified in Chinese, e.g. 'I bought the books' would be translated as 'I bought those books' i.e. 我買了那些書. The object of a verb may be specified in a number of ways:
a) numeral + classifier: 我買了一本書。
b) demonstrative or interrogative adjective: 我買了那本書；你買了什麼書?
c) pronoun modifier: 我買了他的房子。
d) complex adjectival modifiers: 他買了我想買的房子。

Pronouns and interrogative pronouns are already specific and cannot be made more specific and can be used in place of a specified object in this pattern. Also, when specification of the object is implied in Chinese, the suffix *le* can be used, e.g. 'He sold his house' is 他賣了房子。

**2.** SUBJECT + VERB + SUFFIX *le* + UNSPECIFIED OBJECT

When specification of the object does not occur and is not implied, the sentence must be completed by the addition of:
a) The modal *le*, e.g. 'They have gone home' is 他們回(了)家了. Usually the suffix *le* is omitted as the main point of emphasis is the new situation and not the completion of the action.
b) Another clause. The second action can only take place after the completion of the first. Usually a sequ-

# NOTES ON GRAMMAR

ence indicator, e.g. *jiù* 就 is used to introduce the following clause.

We will go shopping after classes. 我們下了課就去買東西。

We will go home after we have something to eat. 我們吃了東西就回家。

**3. SUBJECT + VERB (+ SUFFIX *le*) + MODAL *le***

In sentences without an object the aspect of the new situation is stronger than the aspect of completion of the action. Hence the suffix *le* is absorbed by the modal particle *le*: 他上去（了）了 ⟶ 他上去了。

**4. SUBJECT + VERB + SUFFIX *le* + QUANTIFIED OBJECT + MODAL *le***

This pattern is used to show that the general action is still progressing:

Teacher asked us to buy two writing brushes; I bought one today and I shall buy another tomorrow. 老師叫我們買兩枝毛筆；我今天買了一枝了，明天還要買一枝。

**5.** The negative sentence is formed by using *méi* 沒 or *méiyou* 沒有 before the verb.

上個星期我沒(有)上課。

去年他沒(有)來。

我沒(有)買水果。

他沒(有)去。

我沒(有)看見他。

**6.** The interrogative sentence may be formed by adding the interrogative particle *ma* 嗎 at the end of the sentence or by using the alternative question pattern:

你買了那本書了嗎？

他喝了那兩杯酒了嗎？

他吃了那包水果了嗎？

他早上來了沒有？

他們昨天去了沒有？

# EXERCISES

**A.** Translate into Chinese:

1.   He came early today.
2.   I did not see him yesterday.
3.   There are 30 days in June.
4.   We will go home after we do the shopping.
5.   I have already bought two books.
6.   I did not hear you speak.
7.   Did he come early last week?
8.   Have they gone home?

**B.** Translate into English:

1.   我剛才買了兩條魚。
2.   他告訴我他買了東西就回家。
3.   去年他在英國教中文。
4.   上個星期我還在日本。
5.   他常常晚上來。
6.   我看見的鉛筆都很貴，我只買了一枝。
7.   那兩天我沒有聽見他唱那首歌。
8.   今天上午他來得很晚。
9.   我上個星期買的水果還在這兒。
10.  有些學生不喜歡用這個新方法。

**LESSON TEN**

# VOCABULARY

| | | | |
|---|---|---|---|
| 1. zài | 在 | | to be in, at, on; indicates continuing action |
| 2. zhèngzài | 正在 | | just in the process of |
| 3. lǐ | 裏 | 里 | in, inside |
| 4. shàng | 上 | | on, above, up |
| 5. lǐbian(r) | 裏邊（兒） | 里边（儿） | inside; also *lǐmiàn* 裏面 |
| 6. shàngbian(r) | 上邊（兒） | 上边（儿） | above, up there; also *shàngmiàn* 上面 |
| 7. xiàbian(r) | 下邊（兒） | 下边（儿） | below, under, down there; also *xià-miàn* 下面 |
| 8. qiánbian(r) | 前邊（兒） | 前边（儿） | front, in front, in front of; also *qián-miàn* 前面 |
| 9. hòubian(r) | 後邊（兒） | 后边（儿） | back, behind, at the back of; also *hòu-miàn* 後面 |
| 10. wàibian(r) | 外邊（兒） | 外边（儿） | outside; also *wàimiàn* 外面 |
| 11. zuǒbian(r) | 左邊（兒） | 左边（儿） | left(side) |
| 12. yòubian(r) | 右邊（兒） | 右边（儿） | right(side) |
| 13. dōngbian(r) | 東邊（兒） | 东边（儿） | east, in the east |
| 14. nánbian(r) | 南邊（兒） | 南边（儿） | south, in the south |
| 15. xībian(r) | 西邊（兒） | 西边（儿） | west, in the west |
| 16. běibian(r) | 北邊（兒） | 北边（儿） | north, in the north |
| 17. lóushang | 樓上 | 楼上 | upstairs |
| 18. lóuxia | 樓下 | 楼下 | downstairs |
| 19. zhōngjiàn(r) | 中間（兒） | 中间（儿） | in the middle; in between |
| 20. mén | 門 | 门 | door (cl.*shàn* 扇) |
| 21. zhuōzi | 桌子 | | table (cl. 張) |
| 22. bǎ | 把 | | classifier for chairs and other objects which may be grasped in the hand e.g. knife, fan |
| 23. yǐzi | 椅子 | | chair (cl. 把) |
| 24. dìshang | 地上 | | (on the) floor, (on the) ground |
| 25. chéngli | 城裏 | 城里 | (in the) city |
| 26. chéngshì | 城市 | | city |
| 27. xiāngxia | 鄉下 | 乡下 | (in the) countryside |

# VOCABULARY

| 28. | jiēshang | 街上 | (on the) street |
| 29. | ne | 呢 | modal particle indicating a continuing action |
| 30. | zhe | 着 | verbal suffix indicating aspect of continuing state or result of an action |
| 31. | fàng | 放 | to place, to put |
| 32. | tǎng | 躺 | to lie down (of animate objects) |
| 33. | chuáng | 床 | bed (cl. 張 ) |

# NOTES ON GRAMMAR

## Compass Directions

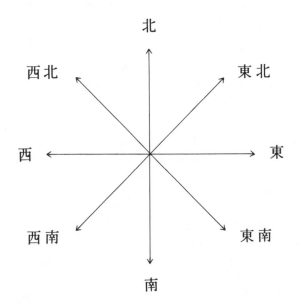

## Location

**1.** Location can be expressed by adding *zhèr/zhèli* or *nàr/nàli* ( 這兒/ 這裏 or 那兒/ 那裏) to nouns and pronouns to form sentences of the type:

The houses over there (where he is living) are all good. 他那兒的房子都好 .

It is very good here (where we are). 我們這兒很好。

**2.** Construction with *zài* 在 : *Zài* means 'in', 'at', 'on', 'to be in (a place)', 'to be on (something)' e.g. *Tā zài zhèr* 他在這兒'He is here'. When the object of *zài* is a noun or pronoun, e.g. 'house' or 'us', a specific location indicator, e.g. 'in front of', 'behind', is also required. The particle *de* 的 is understood to stand between the object and the specific location indicator although it is often omitted, e.g.

He is on my left. 他在我(的)左邊 。

They are at the back of the house. 他們在房子(的)後面 。

His house is in front of the school. 他的房子在學校(的)前邊 。

Points to observe when using specific location indicators:

a) Specific location indicators are generally disyllabic, e.g. *wàibianr* 外邊兒, *zuǒbianr* 左邊兒.

b) The monosyllabic specific location indicators *shang* 上 and *li* 裏 are used for 'on' and 'in' respectively, e.g. 'on the table' is *zài zhuōzi shang* 在桌子上 and 'in the house' is *zài fángzi li* 在房子裏. The disyllabic counterparts of *shang* and *li* i.e. *shàngmiàn* 上面, *shàngbianr* 上邊兒 and *lǐmiàn* 裏面 , *lǐbianr* 裏邊兒 are used for 'top surface', 'top section', 'above' and 'inside of ' respectively, e.g. 'The top of the table is not clean' is *Zhuōzi shàngmiàn bùgānjing* 桌子上面不乾淨 and 'The inside of the house is quite clean' is *Fángzi lǐmiàn hěn gānjing* 房子裏面很乾淨.

c) Some specific location indicators have formed lexical units with their nouns, e.g. *jiēshang* 街上, *chéngli* 城裏.

d) The specific location indicator *li* 裏 is not used with geographical names, e.g. 'He is in China' is *Tā zài Zhōngguó* 他在中國 .

e) The specific location indicator *li* 裏 may be omitted when the place word following *zài* denotes the names of buildings, institutions and organizations etc. For example, 'He is reading in the library' is *Tā zài túshūguǎn kànshū* 他在圖書館看書 . When *li*, *lǐmiàn* or *lǐbianr* are used in such sentences, 'in' or 'inside' is emphasized.

**3.** The prepositional use of *zài* 在 : When *zài* is used as a preposition the whole adverbial phrase expressing location is placed before the verb.

SUBJECT + *zài* + NOUN/PRONOUN + SPECIFIC LOCATION INDICATOR + VERB (+ OBJECT)

他在樓上看書 。

他們在鄉下教書 。

我們在城裏買東西 。

小孩子在桌子下面看書 。

When location and time phrases occur together, the time phrase precedes the location phrase. If greater emphasis is on the time phrase, it may precede the subject of the sentence.

# NOTES ON GRAMMAR

## The Aspect of Continuing Action *zài* 在, *zhèngzài* 正在 **and** *ne* 呢

In Chinese the simple use of verbs can indicate the continuous tense of an English verb, e.g. 'He is teaching in China' is *Tā zài Zhōngguó jiāoshū* 他在中國教書. However, in Chinese the aspect of an action is important. Therefore if one wishes to stress the aspect of a continuing action it is shown in one of the following ways:

**1.** By the use of *zài* meaning '(still) ... -ing', or *zhèngzài* for greater emphasis: SUBJECT + *zài/zhèngzài* + VERB + OBJECT

What is he doing?　他在做什麼？
He is reading a book.　他在看書。
He is having dinner.　他在吃晚飯。

The above construction can refer to action that was or is in progress at a particular time, e.g. 'Yesterday when I went to his home he was having dinner' is *Zuótian wǒ qù tā jiā de shíhou tā zhèngzài chī wǎnfàn* 昨天我去他家的時候,他正在吃晚飯. The continuous aspect is not often used in reference to the future; when it is, the use of an adverb such as *yídìng* 一定 ('certainly') is necessary, e.g. 'If you go at 12 o'clock he will (certainly) be eating lunch' is *Yàoshi nǐ shí'èr diǎnzhōng qù tā yídìng zài chīfàn* 要是你十二點鐘去,他一定在吃飯. (*yàoshi* 要是, meaning 'if').

**2.** The modal particle *ne* may be placed at the end of a sentence containing *zài* or *zhèngzài* to heighten the aspect of continuation. In an established context, the *zài* or *zhèngzài* may be omitted and *ne* will serve to convey the aspect of continuation.

'Haven't you read today's paper?' 'I'm reading it right now!' 你還沒看今天的報紙嗎？ 我正在看呢！
'What are you doing?' 'Reading.'　你在做什麼呢？　看書呢！

**3.** The negative form of continuing action: 'He is not reading' is *Tā búzài kànshū* 他不在看書.

## Continuing State or Result of an Action *zhe* 着

**1.** The verbal suffix *zhe* is used to indicate a state or result which persists and continues after the initial action. It expresses state and not action, i.e. it describes the result of an action.

He is looking angrily at me.　他生氣地看着我。
He is lying on the floor.　他在地上躺着。
I am holding a book.　我拿着一本書。
The students are listening happily.　學生高興地聽着。
Some old books were lying on the table. 桌子上放着一些舊書。

**2.** Sometimes a verb with *zhe* is used as an adverbial adjunct which describes the manner of an action. The pattern is: X while doing A *zhe* does B, e.g. 'I eat standing up' is *Wǒ zhànzhe chīfàn* 我站着吃飯. In other words there are two actions going on at the same time, the first of which describes the manner of the second. Nothing can come between the verb and the suffix *zhe*. *Zhe* cannot take a complement and if there is an object, it follows *zhe*.

Those two students are reading whilst lying on the bed. 那兩個學生在床上躺着看書。
He does not wish to eat whilst sitting down.　他不想坐着吃飯。

**3.** The difference between the aspect of continuation of the action of the verb using *zài* or *zhèngzài* and that of continuation of the action after the initial action expressed by the use of the verbal suffix *zhe* may be seen by comparing the following sentences:

He is getting (fetching) a newspaper. 他在拿報。
He is holding a newspaper.　他拿着報。

At times there is little difference between a continuing action and the state of an action after it begins. In such cases the *zài* construction may be used together with *zhe*. When this occurs, the modal *ne* is generally used, e.g. *Wǒmen zhèngzài xiězhe ne* 我們正在寫着呢, 'We are in the process of writing it!'

**4.** In the negative sentence *méi(you)* is used:
I was not holding it.　我沒(有)拿着。
Were you not seated?　你沒(有)坐着嗎？

---

# EXERCISES

**A.** Translate into Chinese:
1. Whose are the things lying on the bed?
2. The houses on the south side of the city are expensive.
3. They are at home reading.
4. The children are on the street playing.
5. He still has not told me!
6. There is no library there (where they are).

**B.** Translate into English:
1. 他們還在地上躺着嗎？
2. 桌子上放着什麼？
3. 桌子上放着兩個杯子。
4. 他們在街上慢慢地走着。
5. 小孩子在外面玩着。
6. 城東邊的房子都很舊。
7. 床下邊的東西不是我的。
8. 學校前邊的學生是英國人。

**LESSON ELEVEN**

# VOCABULARY

| | | | | |
|---|---|---|---|---|
| 1. | Běijīng | 北京 | | Beijing (Peking) |
| 2. | Shànghǎi | 上海 | | Shanghai |
| 3. | Nánjīng | 南京 | | Nanjing (Nanking) |
| 4. | Guǎngzhōu | 廣州 | 广州 | Guangzhou (Canton) |
| 5. | dào | 到 | | to arrive; to reach |
| 6. | cóng | 從 | 从 | from |
| 7. | lí | 離 | 离 | to be separated in distance |
| 8. | líkāi | 離開 | 离开 | to leave (place, person) |
| 9. | yuǎn | 遠 | 远 | distant, far |
| 10. | jìn | 近 | | close, near |
| 11. | gōnglǐ | 公里 | | kilometre |
| 12. | zhǐ | 隻 | 只 | classifier for boats, parts of the body and most birds and animals |
| 13. | chuán | 船 | | boat, ship (cl. 隻, 條, sǒu 艘 ) |
| 14. | fēijǐ | 飛機 | 飞机 | aeroplane (cl. jià 架 ) |
| 15. | qìchē | 汽車 | 汽车 | motor car (cl. liàng 輛, bù 部 ) |
| 16. | huǒchē | 火車 | 火车 | train (cl. liè 列 ) |
| 17. | diànchē | 電車 | 电车 | tram, trolley car (cl. 輛 ) |
| 18. | qí | 騎 | 骑 | to ride (astride) |
| 19. | mǎ | 馬 | 马 | horse (cl. pǐ 匹 ) |
| 20. | zìxíngchē | 自行車 | 自行车 | bicycle (cl. 輛, 部 ) |
| 21. | niú | 牛 | | cow (cl. tóu 頭 ) |
| 22. | kāi | 開 | 开 | to open, to operate/drive a machine or vehicle |
| 23. | néng | 能 | | to be able (to) |
| 24. | huì | 會 | 会 | to be able (to) i.e. to know how (to); to know |
| 25. | kéyi | 可以 | | to be able (to) |
| 26. | kěnéng | 可能 | | possibly, might |
| 27. | yīnggāi | 應該 | 应该 | ought, should, to be obliged to |
| 28. | xǐwàng | 希望 | | hope, to hope |
| 29. | gǎn | 敢 | 敢 | to dare (to) |

# VOCABULARY

| 30. | yuànyi | 願意 | 愿意 | to be willing (to) |
|---|---|---|---|---|
| 31. | pà | 怕 | | to be afraid (of) |
| 32. | zhèngxiǎng | 正想 | | just about to |
| 33. | zhèngyào | 正要 | | just about to |
| 34. | duō(me) | 多(麼) | 多(么) | how? (i.e. to what extent) |
| 35. | búyòng | 不用 | | no need to, do not have to |
| 36. | búbì | 不必 | | no necessity to, do not have to |
| 37. | róngyì | 容易 | | easy |
| 38. | nán | 難 | 难 | difficult |

# NOTES ON GRAMMAR

### The Prepositional Use of *dào* 到, *cóng* 從, *zuò* 坐, *qí* 騎 and *lí* 離

*Dào, cóng, zuò, qí* and *lí* are prepositions (coverbs) which linked with their objects form constructions which may then be used as adverbial modifiers of the main verb; as adverbial modifiers, they will stand before the verb.

**1.** Motion to a place: While motion to a place may be expressed with the simple construction using *lái* 來 or *qù* 去, e.g. 'I am going to Shanghai' is *Wǒ yào qù Shànghǎi* 我要去上海 and 'He often comes here' is *Tā chángcháng lái zhèr* 他常常來這兒, a prepositional construction using *dào* is also commonly used. In this construction 來 and 去 are pronounced in the neutral tone.
SUBJECT + *dào* + PLACE WORD + VERB (*lai/qu*)
He is going to Shanghai. 他要到上海去。
He does not want to go to Guangzhou. 他不想到廣州去。
He often comes to Nanjing. 他常常到南京來。

**2.** Motion from a place:
SUBJECT + *cóng* + PLACE WORD + VERB (*lai/qu*)
Do not enter from the left side. 不要從左邊進來。
He will come from the school. 他要從學校來。

**3.** Motion from one place to another:
a) SUBJECT + *cóng* + PLACE WORD(1) + VERB (*lái/qù*) + PLACE WORD(2)
He will go from Guangzhou to Nanjing. 他要從廣州去南京。
They will come here from Beijing. 他們要從北京來這兒。
b) SUBJECT + *cóng* + PLACE WORD(1) + *dào* + PLACE WORD(2) + VERB (*lai/qu*)

He says that he will go to Shanghai from Guangzhou.
他說他要從廣州到上海去。
He does not want to go to Nanjing from Shanghai.
他不想從上海到南京去。

**4.** Purpose or reason for motion to or from a place is expressed by using two verbal constructions in succession, the second one indicating the purpose. When the *dào...lai/qu* construction is used, the verb *lai/qu* has the additional function of connecting the two verbal constructions.
a) SUBJECT + VERB (*lái/qù*) + PLACE WORD + VERB (+ OBJECT)
He goes to the library to read. 他去圖書館看書。
They are coming to Guangzhou to teach English. 他們要來廣州教書。
b) SUBJECT + *dào* + PLACE WORD + VERB (*lai/qu*) + VERB (+ OBJECT)
I do not want to go to Shanghai to work. 我不想到上海去工作。
I have come here to eat a meal. 我到這兒來吃飯。

**5.** Travel in, on, or by vehicle or animal: *zuò* and *qí* may be used to form prepositional constructions with their objects (vehicle or animal) to express mode of travel. *Zuò* (to sit) is used with vehicles where one is seated as opposed to riding astride. *Qí* (to sit astride) is used for travelling on bicycles and animals.
a) SUBJECT + *zuò* + VEHICLE (where one is seated) + VERB
He goes by car. 他坐汽車去。
They often come by tram. 他們常常坐電車來。
He does not want to go by aeroplane. 他不想坐飛機去。

b) SUBJECT + *qí* + VEHICLE (bicycle/animal on which one sits astride) + VERB

He does not often come by horse. 他不常常騎馬來。

He does not want to ride a bicycle there. 他不想騎自行車到那兒去。

**6.** Distance is shown between two entities or places by using *lí* in a prepositional construction.

A + *lí* + B + MEASURE PHRASE

How far is Shanghai from Beijing? 上海離北京多遠？

It is quite far from here. 離這兒很遠。

How far is your new house from your old one? It is not far, only two kilometres. 你的新房子離舊的多遠？ 不遠，只有兩公里。

## Auxiliary Verbs with Special Usages

**1.** *Néng* 能 and *kéyi* 可以 'can', may express ability, consent by circumstances or permission and may be used interchangeably in affirmative sentences. In present day usage, *kéyi* is generally not used with a negative, so that 'cannot' is generally *bùnéng* 不能.

Affirmative:
He can tell you. 他可以／能告訴你。
We can all go. 我們都可以／能去。

Negative:
He cannot tell you. 他不能告訴你。
None of us can go. 我們都不能去。

Interrogative:
Can you come? 你可以／能來嗎？
Can you all come? 你們都可以／能來嗎？
Can you tell me? 你可以／能告訴我嗎？

**2.** *Huì* 會 when used as a full verb means 'to know', i.e. to possess acquired knowledge or skill for performing something, e.g. 'Do you know Japanese?' is *Nǐ huìbuhuì Rìwén?* 你會不會日文？ and 'No, I only know Chinese' is *Búhuì, wǒ zhǐ huì Zhōngwén* 不會，我只會中文.

a) As an auxiliary verb *huì* may mean 'can' (i.e. know how to):

Can you drive a car? 你會不會開汽車？
I can only ride a bicycle. 我只會騎自行車。
He can already write five hundred Chinese characters. 他己經會寫五百個漢字了。

b) *Huì* may also mean 'could possibly', 'would probably' or 'will certainly':

He will certainly come today. 他今天一定會來。
It is not likely that he will come today. 他今天不會來。
He may come tomorrow. 他明天可能會來。

**3.** *Yào* 要 and *xiǎng* 想: When *yào* is used as a full verb it means 'to want' while *xiǎng* means 'to think' as a full verb. *Yào* and *xiǎng* are used as auxiliary verbs in the following ways:

a) *Yào* and *xiǎng* may be used interchangeably as auxiliary verbs with the meaning of 'to want to', 'to wish to' in affirmative sentences, e.g. 'I want to go to the city to shop' may be *Wǒ xiǎng dào chéngli qu mǎi dōngxi* 我想到城裏去買東西, or *Wǒ yào dào chéngli qu mǎi dōngxi* 我要到城裏去買東西. However, in negative sentences expressing the meaning 'do not want to' *bùxiǎng* 不想 is preferred, e.g. 'We do not want to go in' is *Wǒmen bùxiǎng jìnqu* 我們不想進去, and 'They do not want to come out' is *Tāmen bùxiǎng chūlai* 他們不想出來.

b) *Yào* may be used as an auxiliary verb in affirmative sentences to express necessity or obligation, i.e. 'must', 'should', 'have to'. Used in this way it is commonly preceded by the adverb *yídìng* 一定 (certainly). In negative sentences, however, the meaning of 'do not have to' (i.e. do not need to) is expressed with *búyòng* 不用 while 'do not have to' (i.e. no necessity to, not essential that) is expressed with *búbì* 不必.

I must buy some fruit. 我一定要買一些水果。
You must read those two books. 你一定要看那兩本書。
You do not have to come tomorrow (i.e. there is no need for you to come tomorrow.) 你明天不用來了。

You do not have to tell him. (i.e. there is no necessity for you to tell him.) 你不必告訴他。

c) *Yào* may be used in affirmative sentences as an auxiliary verb to express future action, i.e. 'will', 'shall', 'is/are going to'. The expression *búyào* 不要 is not used as the negative of the auxiliary in this sense. Instead, either the main verb is negated or *búhuì* 不會 is used when improbability is implied. Therefore the alternative type interrogative sentence does not use *yàobuyao* 要不要 to express future action but *huìbuhui* 會不會 when improbability is implied or else the simple use of positive and negative forms of the main verb.

I shall be teaching next year. 我明年要教書了。
I shall not be working next month. 我下個月不工作。
Will they be coming next week? 他們下個星期會不會來？

d) The negative of the auxiliary verb *yào* i.e. *búyào* 不要 generally expresses prohibition, e.g. 'Do not tell him!' is *Búyào gàosu tā* 不要告訴他. *Bù* 不 of course occurs with the full verb *yào* in sentences such as 'I do not want coffee' *Wǒ búyào kāfēi* 我不要咖啡。

**4.** *Zhèngxiǎng* 正想 and *zhèngyào* 正要 are used interchangeably to express immediate action, i.e. 'just about to', 'just thinking of':

I was just about to go to his place. 我正想到他兒去。
I was just thinking of having something to eat. 我正要吃一點兒東西。
When he arrived I was just about to go to the library. 他來的時候，我正想到圖書館去。

**5.** *Yīnggāi* 應該 means 'ought to', 'should' and refers to demand or necessity dictated by reason or duty.
We should first discuss this matter. 我們應該先討論這個問題。
You should go home often. 你應該常常回家。

# EXERCISES

**A.** Translate into Chinese:
1. His old house is close to the school.
2. Beijing is not near Guangzhou.
3. He is unwilling to travel by boat.
4. They are afraid of you.
5. I was just about to tell you.
6. Can they drive a car?
7. That boat often goes from Nanjing to Beijing.
8. I do not dare to travel by aeroplane.
9. Teacher said that we cannot go.
10. You ought to tell them.

**B.** Translate into English:

1. 他不願意到南京去教書。
2. 我明年要去鄉下工作。
3. 他要從北京到這兒來工作。
4. 他工作的地方離這兒很近。
5. 我希望後年到法國去。
6. 你們不用坐火車去，我有汽車。
7. 老師説我不能去。
8. 你的新房子離他那兒多遠？

**LESSON TWELVE**

# VOCABULARY

| | | | | |
|---|---|---|---|---|
| 1. dì | 第 | | | ordinal prefix |
| 2. ...de hěn | 得很 | | | very, extremely |
| 3. kěshi | 可是 | | | but, however |
| 4. dànshi | 但是 | | | but, however |
| 5. búguo | 不過 | 不过 | | only, but, however |
| 6. juéde | 覺得 | 觉得 | | to feel, perceive |
| 7. yìsi | 意思 | | | meaning |
| 8. yǒu yìsi | 有意思 | | | to be meaningful, to be interesting |
| 9. bǎ | 把 | | | preposition used in disposal constructions |
| 10. zǔguó | 祖國 | 祖国 | | homeland (lit. land of one's ancestors) |
| 11. sòng | 送 | | | to give as a present, to escort to |
| 12. jièshào | 介紹 | 介绍 | | to introduce |
| 13. tuǐ | 推 | | | to push |
| 14. lā | 拉 | | | to drag, to pull |
| 15. bǎ... dǎkāi | 把...打開 | 把...打开 | | to open (door, window, box etc.) |
| 16. bǎ... guānqilai | 把...關起來 | 把...关起来 | | to close (door, window, box etc.) |
| 17. jiějué | 解決 | | | to resolve, to settle |
| 18. wàngle | 忘了 | | | to forget |
| 19. xiāoxi | 消息 | | | news, information |
| 20. nèiróng | 内容 | | | contents (of a matter, story etc.) |
| 21. jiàoyù | 教育 | | | education |
| 22. jīngjì | 經濟 | 经济 | | economics |
| 23. gōngyè | 工業 | 工业 | | industry |
| 24. shāngyè | 商業 | 商业 | | commerce |
| 25. nóngyè | 農業 | 农业 | | agriculture |
| 26. wénxué | 文學 | 文学 | | literature |
| 27. kēxué | 科學 | 科学 | | science |
| 28. lìshǐ | 歷史 | 历史 | | history |
| 29. yánjiu | 研究 | | | to carry out research; pronounced *yánjiū* when used as a noun |
| 30. gùshì | 故事 | | | story, plot (of a novel etc.) |

# NOTES ON GRAMMAR

## The Ordinal Prefix *dì* 第

The ordinal prefix *dì* is used to form ordinal numbers: first, *dìyǐ* 第一; second, *dì'èr* 第二; ninth, *dìjiǔ* 第九, etc. When an ordinal number is followed by a noun (or when a noun is implied) a classifier must be used, e.g 'The first house is old' is *Dìyǐ suǒ fángzi hěn jiù* 第一所房子很舊; if the topic under discussion pertains to a number of particular houses one might say 'The first is old' i.e. *Dìyǐ suǒ hěn jiù* 第一所很舊. In cases of nouns which are themselves measure words no classifier is used, e.g 'the next day' is *dì'èr tiān* 第二天, 'the third time' is *dìsān cì* 第三次 and the 'the third year' is *dìsān nián* 第三年. The prefix is not used when specified dates are given, e.g. 26th June 1980 is *yījiǔbālíng nián liùyuè èrshiliù rì* 一九八〇年六月二十六日.

Whose is the third car? 第三輛汽車是誰的？
This is the nineteenth room. 這是第十九間屋子；這間屋子是第十九間。
Who is the fifth person? 第五個人是誰？
This is the first time I have been to Guangzhou. 這是我第一次到廣州來。

## The Pretransitive Construction Using *bǎ* 把

*Bǎ* is a preposition used in a sentence-type called the disposal form or the pretransitive construction. The pattern is:
SUBJECT + *bǎ* + OBJECT + VERB + OTHER ELEMENT(S)
In this construction the object of *bǎ* is also the object of the main verb. As the basic meaning of *bǎ* is to grasp, to seize or to hold, sentences using the disposal form imply that the object is 'seized' (either in a physical or abstract sense) and its state or position changed by the subject of the sentence. The preposition *jiāng* 將 may be used interchangeably with *bǎ* in a pretransitive construction, however it is not as widely used as *bǎ*.

The *bǎ* construction is used under the following circumstances:

**1.** When a change in the position of the object is described, as in the case of verbs with directional complements of the type 'He took out the money' *Tā bǎ qián náchulai le* 他把錢拿出來了.

**2.** When a change in the state of the object is described as in the case of verbs with resultative complements (see Lesson Fifteen) of the type 'Please take the books away' *Qǐng nǐ bǎ shū nákāi* 請你把書拿開.

**3.** When a sentence contains both a direct and indirect object. In this type of sentence, *bǎ* precedes the direct object and the indirect object is placed after the verb, e.g. 'He gives me the money' is *Tā bǎ qián gěi wǒ* 他把錢給我.

**4.** When one wishes to emphasize the object, the *bǎ* construction allows the object to stand before the verb, hence giving emphasis to the object. In the sentence *Qǐng nǐ bǎ zhèběn shū gěi wǒ* 請你把這本書給我 (Please give me this book) *zhèběn shū* 這本書 is emphasized more than in the sentence *Qǐng nǐ gěi wǒ zhèběn shū* 請你給我這本書. This subtle shade of difference is often not obvious in the English translation.

**5.** The *bǎ* construction must be used when a sentence contains a complement and other elements which are closely linked with the verb and cannot be separated from it, e.g 'He put the things on the table' *Tā bǎ dōngxi fàngzai zhuōzi shang* 他把東西放在桌子上.

When using the *bǎ* construction the following points should be observed:
a) There is usually a further element following the verb, such as a particle, a complement, an indirect object or else the verb itself must be reduplicated (see Lesson Seventeen).
Directional complement:
Bring the wine! 把酒拿來！
Modal particle *le* 了 indicating perfective sense:
He has sold my house. 他把我的房子賣了。
He has forgotten my name. 他把我的名字忘了.
Resultative complement:
Push aside the chair. 把椅子推開。
Put my money on the floor. 把我的錢放在地上。
Indirect object:
He told me the news. 他把消息告訴了我。
He gave me those old things. 他把那些舊東西給了我。
Complement of degree:
You are selling those things too cheaply. 你把那些東西賣得太便宜。
Verb repeated:
Please open the door a little. 請你把門開開。
b) *Bǎ* always takes a definite object; even if no specific modifier is used a definite object is always implied. The reason for this is that the *bǎ* construction makes definite and emphasizes the object by transposing it in front of the verb. Compare: 'He gives me money' *Tā gěi wǒ qián* 他給我錢 and 'He gives me the money' *Tā bǎ qián gěi wǒ* 他把錢給我. Other examples:
He has already given me the book. 他已經把書給我了。
He has already told me the contents of the story. 他已經把故事的內容告訴了我了。
They immediately told me the news. 他們立刻把消息告訴了我了。
He has already put the things in the car. 他已經把東西放在汽車裏面了。
c) In many cases the *bǎ* construction is dispensable and a simpler construction is possible. However, for the sake of clarity and emphasis the *bǎ* construction is preferable. Some *bǎ* constructions contain complements and other elements which are closely related to the verb and there is no alternative construction for these sentences. For example:
(i) Where *dào* 到 and *zài* 在 follow the verb as resultative

# NOTES ON GRAMMAR

complements (see Lesson Seventeen):

He put the book in front of me. 他把書放在我的面前了。

He placed the cup of tea in front of her. 他把那杯茶放在她的面前了。

They pushed the chair to the left side of the door. 他們把椅子推到門的左邊了。

I escorted the child to the school. 我把孩子送到學校去了。

(ii) Where a complement e.g. *cì* 次 'time(s)' occurs with the direct object, the complement will of course follow the verb:

He told me the news three times. 他把這個消息告訴了我三次。

He only wrote your name once. 他只把你的名字寫了一次。

d) The *bǎ* construction is generally used when both an indirect object and a direct object occur with *gěi* 給 used to introduce the direct object. (See Lesson Seventeen)

I have already introduced him to the teacher. 我已經把他介紹給老師了。

He gave those things to me (as a present). 他把那些東西送給了我。

e) Some verbs which have no sense of disposal cannot be used in *bǎ* constructions e.g. *lái* 來 , *qù* 去 , *dào* 到 , *xǐhuan* 喜歡 , *kànjian* 看見 , *zhīdao* 知道 and *juéde* 覺得 One cannot say #*Wǒ bǎ shū kànjian le* 我把書看見了 for seeing is an involuntary action and does not dispose. However, one can say *Nǐ yào bǎ shìqing kànqīngchu* 你要把事情看清楚 'You must look at the matter until it becomes clear' because one can voluntarily look at something.

# EXERCISES

**A.** Translate into Chinese:

1. He wrote his name very small.
2. Do not put my bag under the table.
3. He wrote his name on the left side of mine.
4. He refuses to introduce his friend to us.
5. Please take those old things outside.
6. Those three students are extremely tall.
7. The tenth one is yours.
8. Give these two chairs to him (as presents).
9. They pushed his car to the back of the house.
10. I have already forgotten his name.

**B.** Translate into English:

1. 張： 李文英，你什麼時候開始學習中國文學的？

2. 李： 去年。

3. 張： 你喜歡不喜歡學習中國文學？

4. 李： 非常喜歡。研究中國文學很不容易，學習漢字又很難。因為我四歲的時候就離開了祖國，我把很多漢字都忘了。我在澳大利亞的時候已經開始學習經濟，可是覺得沒有意思。前年一位朋友把幾本討論中國文學的書送給我。我想立刻回到中國來。不過那個時候我不能離開澳大利亞。去年二月我第一次回到祖國。

**C.** Answer the following questions in Chinese:

1. 李文英是什麼時候回祖國的？
2. 這是不是他第一次回祖國？
3. 李文英喜歡學習中國文學嗎？
4. 李文英覺得學經濟有意思嗎？
5. 李文英為什麼把很多漢字都忘了？

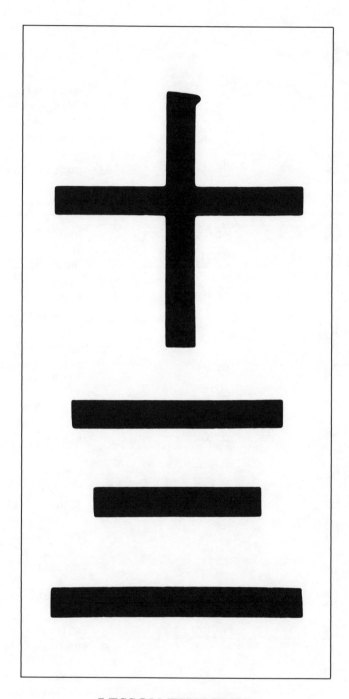

**LESSON THIRTEEN**

# VOCABULARY

| | | | |
|---|---|---|---|
| 1. huòzhě | 或者 | | maybe, perhaps; either...or... (where both alternatives could be posssible) |
| 2. háishi | 還是 | 还是 | either...or... (where a choice is to be made) |
| 3. sīxiǎng | 思想 | | ideology, thinking, thought |
| 4. piān | 篇 | | classifier for essay, article, poem, short story, novel etc. |
| 5. xiǎoshuō | 小説 | 小说 | novel, fiction |
| 6. jìnbù | 進步 | 进步 | progress, to progress, progressive |
| 7. luòhòu | 落後 | 落后 | backward |
| 8. fāzhǎn | 發展 | 发展 | to develop, development |
| 9. fādá | 發達 | 发达 | flourishing, prosperous |
| 10. xuānchuán | 宣傳 | 宣传 | to promote (an idea, thinking, ideology etc.); propaganda |
| 11. tíchàng | 提倡 | | to advocate |
| 12. fǎnduì | 反對 | 反对 | to oppose |
| 13. pīpíng | 批評 | 批评 | to criticize |
| 14. zhǔyì | 主義 | 主义 | ideology, -ism |
| 15. zhìdù | 制度 | | system |
| 16. zhèngzhì | 政治 | | politics, political |
| 17. zhèngfǔ | 政府 | | government |
| 18. gémìng | 革命 | | revolution |
| 19. yíyàng | 一樣 | 一样 | to be the same |
| 20. zhème; zème | 這麼 | 这么 | so (to this extent) e.g. 'so good', zhème hǎo 這麼好 |
| 21. nàme; nème | 那麼 | 那么 | so (to that extent) e.g. 'so expensive', nàme guì 那麼貴 |
| 22. bǐ | 比 | | preposition used in comparisons |
| 23. zìjǐ | 自己 | | oneself (i.e. personally) e.g. wǒ zìjǐ 我自己 I myself; tā zìjǐ 他自己 he himself; tāmen zìjǐ 他們自己 they themselves |
| 24. fēng | 封 | | classifier for letter |
| 25. xìn | 信 | | letter |
| 26. yǐngxiǎng | 影響 | 影响 | influence |

# NOTES ON GRAMMAR

## The (*háishi* 還是) ... *háishi* 還是 ... Construction

*Háishi* is an adverb meaning 'still' but may be used in a construction forming an interrogative sentence which will give the meaning 'or' in the sense 'either...or...' where a choice is asked. In the basic construction each alternative is preceded by *háishi* but in practice the first *háishi* is often omitted. At the same time it should be noted that the emphatic *shì* 是 may be used in place of the first *háishi* to give greater emphasis to the first alternative. The effect of the emphatic *shì* in this construction gives the meaning of 'is it a case of...or...'. For example, 'Do you want to buy it or does the teacher want to buy it?' (i.e. Is it a case of your wanting to buy it or the teacher wanting to buy it) is *Shì nǐ yào mǎi háishi lǎoshī yào mǎi?* 是你要買還是老師要買?

In sentences where 'or' is used to give the sense '(either/neither) ...or/nor...VERB', i.e. sentences which do not make a choice between the two alternatives, *huòzhě* 或者 or *huòshì* 或是 is used, e.g. 'I am thinking of going to Nanjing or Shanghai to teach English' is *Wǒ xiǎng qù Nánjīng huòzhě Shànghǎi jiāo Yīngwén* 我想去南京或者上海教英文. In cases where the alternatives are placed in the position of topic, a strongly emphatic sentence results and *dōu* 都 is used to introduce the predicate, e.g. *Zhèzhǒng zhìdù huòzhě nàzhǒng zhìdù dōu bùnéng jiějué zhège wèntí* 這種制度或者那種制度都不能解決這個問題. (Neither this system nor that system can resolve this problem.)

**1.** Expressing a choice between the subjects: (*háishi/shì* +) SUBJECT (1) + PREDICATE + *háishi* + SUBJECT (2) + PREDICATE

Is he going or are you going? 他去,還是你去?
Is this political system progressive or is that political system progressive? 這種政治制度進步,還是那種政治制度進步?
Is this nation's industrial development backward or is that nation's industrial development backward? 這個國家的工業發展落後,還是那個國家的落後?
Will you tell them or will I tell them?
你告訴他們,還是我告訴他們。

**2.** Expressing a choice between predicates: SUBJECT + (*háishi/shì* + ) PREDICATE (1) + *háishi* + PREDICATE (2)

Are you going or not going? 你去還是不去?
Is the government of that nation progressive or backward? 那個國家的政府進步還是落後?
Are such problems numerous or few? 這種問題很多,還是很少?
Does he want to teach literature or history? 他是想教文學,還是想教歷史?
Does he not wish to tell you or is he unable to tell you? 他是不想告訴你,還是不能告訴你?

**3.** Expressing a choice between complements: SUBJECT + *shi* + COMPLEMENT (1) + *háishi* + COMPLEMENT (2)

Are you Chinese or Japanese? 你是中國人,還是日本人?
Are these new (ones) or old (ones)? 這些是新的,還是舊的?
Is this coffee or tea? 這是茶,還是咖啡?

**4.** Expressing an afterthought following a question formed with an interrogative word: QUESTION? + (*háishi* +) ALTERNATIVE (1) + *háishi* + ALTERNATIVE (2)

What do you want to drink? Tea or coffee? 你想喝什麼?茶還是咖啡?
Where do you want to go? To Mr Huang's or to the library? 你想到哪兒去?黃先生那兒還是圖書館?

## Comparisons With Predicative Adjectives

**1.** The *bǐ* 比 construction: *bǐ* is a preposition meaning 'compared with'. It forms a prepositional construction which is used to describe superior degree of comparison e.g. 'He is taller than you' is *Tā bǐ nǐ gāo* 他比你高. The topic under discussion precedes *bǐ* and possesses a superior degree of the adjective than the object of *bǐ*. When *bǐ* is negated contradiction is implied e.g. 'He is not taller than you!' is *Tā bùbǐ nǐ gāo* 他不比你高。

Affirmative:
TOPIC + *bǐ* + OBJECT + ADJECTIVE
My house is cheaper than yours. 我的房子比你的便宜。
This cup is more expensive than that one. 這個杯子比那個貴。

Interrogative:
a) TOPIC + *shìbúshì* + *bǐ* + OBJECT + ADJECTIVE
Is your car larger than his? 你的汽車是不是比他的大?
b) TOPIC + *bǐ* + OBJECT + ADJECTIVE + *ma*
Is this ball-point pen more expensive than that one? 這枝圓珠筆比那枝貴嗎?
Are his students fewer than yours? 他的學生比你的少嗎?

**2.** The *yíyàng* 一樣 construction is used when the topic under discussion is said to possess the same degree of a quality upon comparison e.g. 'He is the same height as the teacher' is *Tā gēn lǎoshī yíyàng gāo* 他跟老師一樣高. The negative forms are used when contradiction is implied e.g. 'I am not the same height as the teacher' is either *Wǒ bùgēn lǎoshī yíyàng gāo* 我不跟老師一樣高 or *Wǒ gēn lǎoshī bùyíyàng gāo* 我跟老師不一樣高. When the interrogative forms are used the question asked is whether the two things being compared possess the same degree of a quality, e.g. 'Are French wines and Australian wines equally expensive?' may be either

# NOTES ON GRAMMAR

*Fǎguó jiǔ gēn Àodàlìyà jiǔ shìbúshi yíyàng guì* 法國酒跟澳大利亞酒是不是一樣貴? or *Fǎguó jiǔ shìbúshi gēn Àodàlìyà jiǔ yíyàng guì* 法國酒是不是跟澳大利亞酒一樣貴?

The affirmative form of the *yíyàng* construction e.g. *Tā gēn lǎoshī yíyàng gāo* (he is the same height as the teacher) is also used to convey the idea A is as ...as B (he is as tall as the teacher):

This type of fish is as cheap as that sort.　這種魚跟那種一樣便宜。

These houses are as old as yours.　這些房子跟你的一樣舊。

This method is as good as the one we used last year. 這個方法跟我們去年用的一樣好。

**3.** The *méiyou* 没有 ...(*nàme* 那麼 /*zhème* 這麼) construction is used to describe inferior degree of comparison, e.g. 'I am not as tall as the teacher' is *Wǒ méiyou lǎoshī nàme gāo* 我没有老師那麼高 . *Nàme* and *zhème* mean 'to such an extent' and are optional in this construction. The affirmative form of this construction is used to express contradiction e.g. 'I am as tall as the teacher' is *Wǒ yǒu lǎoshī gāo* 我有老師高, or *Wǒ yǒu lǎoshī nàme/zhème gāo* 我有老師那麼 / 這麼高。

Negative:
TOPIC + *méiyou* + OBJECT OF COMPARISON (+ *nàme/zhème*) + ADJECTIVE
This house is not as good as that one.　這所房子没有那所好。
The novel he wrote this year is not as good as the one he wrote last year. 他今年寫的小説没有去年寫的好。
My house is not as far away as yours.　我的房子没有你的遠。

Interrogative:
TOPIC + *yǒuméiyou* + OBJECT OF COMPARISON (+ *nàme/zhème*) + ADJECTIVE
Do you have as many as he has? 你有没有他那麼多?
Is this novel as long as that one? 這篇小説有没有那篇長?
Are agricultural problems as numerous as industrial problems? 農業問題有没有工業問題多?

---

# EXERCISES

**A.** Translate into Chinese:
1. Perhaps he is unwilling to tell you.
2. These books are not as expensive as those.
3. My house is not as old as yours.
4. Coffee is cheaper than wine but I would like to drink wine.
5. Ball-point pens are cheaper than writing brushes.
6. Do you want to go in the morning or in the afternoon?
7. His novels all advocate this new type of thinking.
8. Are you afraid that he will criticize this new kind of thinking?
9. These people advocate revolution.
10. The students often criticize the government.
11. Is this system as good as that one?
12. He does not want to go by himself.
13. He says that social revolution and political revolution are equally important.
14. He says that his government is as progressive as ours.

**B.** Translate into English:
1. 這種制度的影響不好。
2. 我不明白這兩種主義。
3. 這篇小説宣傳的思想很落後。
4. 這個國家的政府很進步。
5. 你為什麼反對這種思想?
6. 工業和農業都很發達。
7. 那個時候他已經在宣傳革命思想。
8. 這種主義有没有那種好?
9. 他説他提倡的主義比你提倡的主義進步。
10. 我的汽車比你的小。
11. 喝茶比喝牛奶便宜。
12. 你喜歡喝茶還是喜歡喝咖啡?
13. 老師常常批評我。
14. 他們都反對我到日本去學歷史。他們都説我應該到英國去。
15. 這篇小説的影響不大。

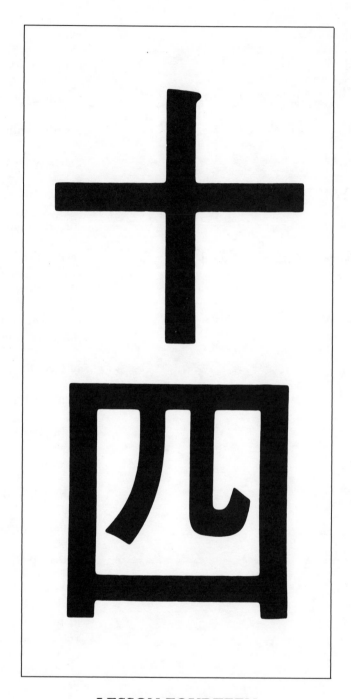

**LESSON FOURTEEN**

# VOCABULARY

| | | | |
|---|---|---|---|
| 1. gèng | 更 | | more |
| 2. zuì | 最 | | most |
| 3. hé | 和 | | with |
| 4. gēn | 跟 | | with |
| 5. gēn...yìqǐ | 跟...一起 | | together with |
| 6. gēn...yìkuàir | 跟...一塊兒 | 跟...一块儿 | together with |
| 7. gōngchǐ | 公尺 | | metre (*gōnglǐ* 公里, kilometre) |
| 8. gōngfēn | 公分 | | centimetre |
| 9. tì | 替 | | for, on behalf of |
| 10. wèile | 爲了 | 为了 | on behalf of, for the sake of, because of (*wèizhe* 爲著 may be used interchangeably with *wèile*) |
| 11. gěi | 給 | 给 | on behalf of, to, for, (i.e. to do something for someone) |
| 12. xiàng | 向 | | to face, to, towards |
| 13. yòng | 用 | | to use, with, by means of |
| 14. shàng | 上 | | to (a place) |
| 15. xǐ | 洗 | | to wash |
| 16. shǒu | 手 | | hand (cl. 隻 ) |
| 17. féizào | 肥皂 | | laundry soap (cl. 塊, 'piece'; 條 'bar') |
| 18. xiāngzào | 香皂 | | bathsoap (cl. 塊; 條) |
| 19. zhǎo | 找 | | to look for |
| 20. jiè | 借 | | a) to borrow. 'To borrow B from A': *xiàng* A *jiè* B, 向 A 借 B. In spoken Chinese *gēn* 跟 may be used interchangeably with *xiàng* in this construction.<br>b) to lend. 'To lend to': *jiègei* 借 給 |
| 21. bìxū | 必須 | 必须 | must |
| 22. xiàyǔ | 下雨 | | to rain (*yǔ* 雨, rain) |
| 23. shuì(jiào) | 睡(覺) | 睡(觉) | to sleep |
| 24. dǎzì | 打字 | | to type (*dǎ* 打 to strike/hit) |
| 25. dǎdiànhuà | 打電話 | 打电话 | to make a telephone call |
| 26. rúguǒ... jiù... | 如果...就... | | if... (then)... |

# NOTES ON GRAMMAR

## Comparisons with the Complement of Degree

**1.** When the *bǐ* 比 construction is used in a sentence containing the complement of degree, *bǐ* and its object may be placed either before the reduplicated form of the verb or before the complement.

a) Where *bǐ* and its object occur before the reduplicated form of the verb:

He speaks Chinese better than I do. 他說中國話比我說得好。

He writes letters more than I do. 他寫信比我寫得多。

He spoke more clearly than you did. 他說話比你說得清楚。

b) When *bǐ* and its object occur before the complement:

He reads French novels faster than I do. 他看法文小說看得比我快。

He writes smaller than I do. 他寫字寫得比我小。

**2.** When the *yíyàng* 一樣 construction is used it precedes the complement in the following ways in affirmative sentences:

a) TOPIC + VERB + *de* + *gēn/hé* + OBJECT OF COMPARISON + (VERB + *de* +) *yíyàng* + COMPLEMENT

He speaks as clearly as the teacher. 他說得跟老師(說得)一樣清楚。

That child eats as much as you do. 那個孩子吃得跟你(吃得)一樣多。

He ate as little as you. 他吃得跟你(吃得)一樣少。

b) TOPIC [subject + verb + object] + VERB + *de* + *gēn/hé* + OBJECT OF COMPARISON + *yíyàng* + COMPLEMENT

He speaks French as well as a Frenchman. 他說法語說得跟法國人一樣好。

He sang that song as well as you did. 他唱那首歌唱得跟你一樣好。

He reads Russian newspapers as quickly as they do. 他看俄文報看得跟他們一樣快。

**3.** The *méiyou* 沒有 ... (*nàme* 那麼/*zhème* 這麼) construction:

Negative patterns:

a) TOPIC + VERB + *de* + *méiyou* + OBJECT OF COMPARISON (+ *nàme/zhème*) + COMPLEMENT

I do not read as quickly as you do. 我看書看得沒有你快。

He did not eat as much fruit as you. 他吃水果吃得沒有你多。

b) TOPIC + *méiyou* + OBJECT OF COMPARISON + VERB + *de* (+ *nàme/zhème*) + COMPLEMENT

He does not write novels as well as you do. 他寫小說沒有你寫得好。

They do not do it as well as we do. 他們沒有我們做得好。

Interrogative patterns:

a) TOPIC + VERB + *de* + *yǒuméiyou* + OBJECT OF COMPARISON (+ *nàme/zhème*) + COMPLEMENT

Does he wash cups as quickly as you? 他洗杯子洗得有沒有你快?

Did he read that novel as quickly as you? 他看那篇小說看得有沒有你快?

Did they use it as slowly as we did? 他們用得有沒有我們慢?

b) TOPIC + *yǒuméiyou* + OBJECT OF COMPARISON + VERB + *de* (+ *nàme/zhème*) + COMPLEMENT

Did he wash his hands as quickly as I did? 他洗手有沒有我洗得快?

Does he type as well as you? 他打字有沒有你打得好?

Does he drink as much coffee as I do? 他喝咖啡有沒有我喝得多?

## Differences and Varying Degrees of Difference in Comparisons

Differences and varying degrees of difference in comparison may be expressed by the use of comparative and superlative adverbs or by the use of complements of degree indicating actual quantity (e.g. 'one inch' or 'ten years of age') or qualities such as late or early, many or few. However, a complete sentence of this type demands a comparison either in the actual sentence or in the context.

**1.** The adverbs *gèng* 更 (more), *hái* 還 (still, more), or the superlative *zuì* 最 (most) may stand before a predicative adjective to emphasize degree of difference:

I am very tall but he is taller. 我很高,可是他更高。

He is very tall but you are even taller. 他很高,可是你比他還高。

These cars are all very good but that one is the best. 這些汽車都很好,可是那輛最好。

He is even younger than you. 他比你還年輕。

He came even later than you. 他來得比你還晚。

He writes Japanese even faster than you. 他寫日文比你寫得還快。

**2.** Predicative adjectives may be followed by *yìdiǎnr* 一點兒 and *yìxiē* 一些 to show slight difference whilst the complement of degree ...*de duō* 得多 may be used to show great difference:

You are a little taller than I. 你比我高一點兒。

This pencil is a little longer than that one. 這枝鉛筆比那枝長一點兒。

He has a few more books than I. 他的書比我的多一些。

Your house is a great deal more expensive than his. 你的房子比他的貴得多。

Is he a little taller than you? 他是不是比你高一點兒?

Is he a great deal younger than you? 他是不是比你年輕得多?

**3.** Predicative adjectives may be followed by numerals and measure phrases to show precise difference:

You are three years older than I am. 你比我大三歲。

I am one centimetre taller than he is. 我比他高一公分。

June has one day less than May. 六月比五月少一天。

**4.** Measure words expressing actual difference may be placed after *zǎo* 早 (early), *wǎn* 晚 (late), *duō* 多 (more, many) and *shǎo* 少 (few, less) to show actual difference between the time or result of one action compared with another:

He went five minutes earlier than you. 他比你早去五分鐘。

Did he go one year later than Mr Zhang? 他是不是比張先生晚去一年？

I walked one kilometre more than you. 我比你多走了一公里。

He slept one hour more than I did. 他比我多睡了一個小時。

**5.** Gradual change with the passage of time may be expressed by using the *bǐ* construction as an adverbial modifier in the following ways:

These sorts of problems gradually (i.e. day by day) increased. 這種問題一天比一天多。

Year by year his letters became fewer. 他寫的信一年比一年少。

**6.** Change with passage of time may be expressed by using the *bǐ* construction as an adverbial modifier in the following ways:

He is slower today than he was yesterday. 他今天比昨天慢

He is taller this year than he was last year by two centimetres. 他今年比去年高兩公分。

## Prepositions

A preposition plus its object forms a prepositional phrase which has the function of modifying a verb. Prepositional phrases are therefore adverbial and as such precede the verbs they modify. In previous lessons we have seen the prepositional use of *zài* 在, *qí* 騎, *zuò* 坐, *dào* 到, *cóng* 從, *lí* 離, *bǐ* 比, *bǎ* 把 etc. All prepositions possess original verbal meanings although in some cases they have ceased to function as independent verbs. Because of the basic verbal sense of prepositions, when a prepositional phrase is modified by an adverb or when an auxiliary verb is used, the adverb or auxiliary will precede the preposition and not the main verb of the clause.

**1.** *Gēn* 跟, *hé* 和 and *tóng* 同 are interchangeable when used as prepositions meaning 'with', although *tóng* is not as commonly used as *gēn* and *hé*.

They are unwilling to go with me. 他們不願意跟我去。

He is not likely to go with Zhang Wenying. 他不會跟張文英去。

**2.** *...gēn* 跟 *... yìqǐ* 一起 and *...gēn* 跟 *... yíkuàir* 一塊兒 mean 'together with':

They will be going with me tomorrow. 他們明天跟我一起去。

He is going to Japan with me next week. 他下星期跟我一起到日本去。

**3.** *Shàng* 上 means 'to', 'towards (a place)'. Used as a preposition *shàng* is similiar to *dào* 到 although *dào* is more widely used:

Where are you going? 你上哪兒去？

I am going to the library. 我上圖書館去。

**4.** *Xiàng* 向 or *xiàngzhe* 向着 as a verb means 'to face' e.g. 'My house faces the west' *Wǒde fángzi xiàng xī* 我的房子向西. Used as prepositions *xiàng* and *xiàngzhe* mean 'to' or 'towards'. In speech *cháo(zhe)* 朝 (着) is often used instead of *xiàng(zhe)*. Both are equally common in the written language, e.g. 'They walked towards the school' is *Tāmen cháo/xiàngzhe xuéxiào zǒuqu le* 他們朝/向着學校走去了。

**5.** *Wèile* 為了, *wèizhe* 為着 (or *wèi* 為) may be used to give the meaning 'because of' expressing purpose or reason for action of the verb or adjectival predicate:

Because of this matter we wanted to go home a day earlier. 為了這件事我們想早一天回家。

Because of the children I must go to Nanjing tomorrow. 為了孩子們我必須明天到南京去。

**6.** *Yòng* 用 means 'with', 'by means of', 'using':

I wash my hands with soap. 我用肥皂洗手。

The children often do not wash their hands with soap. 小孩子們常常不用肥皂洗手。

I do not like to write letters with a writing brush. 我不喜歡用毛筆寫信。

**7.** *Gěi* 給 means 'on behalf of', 'to', 'for the benefit of':

Last year he wrote me three letters. 去年他給我寫了三封信。

Has he written that letter for you? (e.g. a reference) 他給你寫了那封信了嗎？

He often goes shopping for me. 他常常給我買東西。

**8.** *Tì* 替 means 'instead of', 'on behalf of', 'for', 'in place of':

I do not like to borrow books on his behalf. 我不喜歡替他借書。

# EXERCISES

**A.** Translate into Chinese:
1. He is walking slowly towards me.
2. He told the children to wash their hands with soap.
3. Please open the door for me.
4. I am tall but Zhang Wenying is even taller.
5. They told us that this is the best method.
6. Xiao Wang is three years older than you.
7. I shall go a month earlier than you.
8. You are a great deal taller than Xiao Wang.
9. This one is a bit longer.
10. He went home a few minutes earlier than you.
11. They all ran quickly towards the back of the house.
12. They want to go with me to the city.
13. Because of the children he still has to work.
14. I do not know how to do it. Please do it for me.
15. Please put those things on the table for me.
16. He does not speak as slowly as you do.
17. He speaks more clearly than you do.
18. The houses on the left side and the houses on the right side are equally expensive.
19. The houses on the west are as expensive as the houses on the east.
20. This new wine is more expensive than the one we drank yesterday.
21. He likes sleeping on the floor, I like sleeping on the bed.

**B.** Translate into English:
1. 他不肯跟我們一起到上海去。
2. 這種水果很好吃，你吃過沒有？
3. 他中文寫得比我好得多。
4. 我在這兒打電話行不行？ 不行，這是老師用的電話。
5. 已經九點了，我要打電話給他。
6. 他跟我借了二十塊錢。
7. 這兩種魚比那種魚貴得多。
8. 你和我說話的時候，不要吃東西！
9. 你必須今天把工作做完。
10. 請你替我把這些舊雜誌都放在地上。

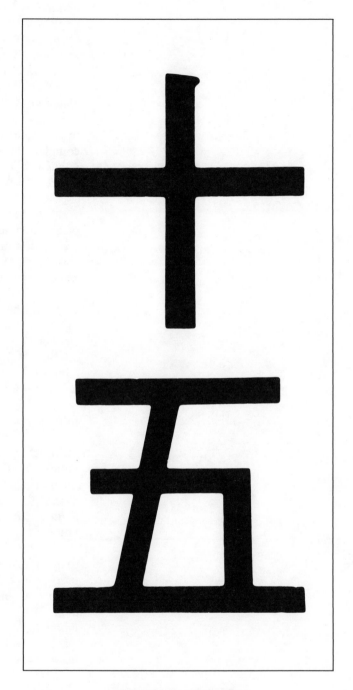

**LESSON FIFTEEN**

# VOCABULARY

1. dào 到 — to arrive, to reach; used as a complement indicating arrival or achievement of an action:
   kàndào 看到 to see
   tīngdào 聽到 to hear
   shuōdào 説到 to speak of/ about
   xiǎngdào 想到 to think of/ about
   jièdào 借到 to borrow
   mǎidào 買到 to buy
   zhǎodào 找到 to find

2. jiàn 見 见 — to perceive with the eyes; used as a complement indicating perception:
   kànjian 看見 to see
   tīngjian 聽見 to hear

3. hǎo 好 — good, to be good/well; used as a complement indicating proper discharge/ completion of an action:
   zuòhǎo 做好 to finish doing
   xiěhǎo 寫好 to finish writing

4. wán 完 — to be finished; used as a complement indicating that an action is finished:
   chīwán 吃完 to finish eating
   hēwán 喝完 to finish drinking
   kànwán 看完 to finish reading
   zuòwán 做完 to finish doing

5. jì 記 记 — to remember

6. zhù 住 — to live in/at; used as a complement to indicate that the result of an action is secured:
   názhù 拿住 to hold on to
   jìzhù 記住 to remember, to bear in mind

7. kāi 開 开 — to open, to drive a mechanized vehicle; used as a complement to indicate departure or separation:
   líkāi 離開 to leave a person or place
   tuīkāi 推開 to push aside/open/away
   nákāi 拿開 to take away
   lākāi 拉開 to drag away

8. huì 會 会 — (refers to learned or acquired abilities or skills) to be able to, to know; used as a complement indicating that understanding or comprehension (acquired or learnt) has been achieved:
   xuéhuì 學會 to have learnt

9. dǒng 懂 — to understand, to comprehend; used as a complement to indicate that comprehension or understanding has resulted from an action:
   kàndǒng 看懂 to understand (on reading)
   tīngdǒng 聽懂 to understand (on hearing)

# VOCABULARY

| 10. | cuò | 錯 | 错 | to be wrong; used as a complement to indicate that an action has been done incorrectly:<br>*kàncuò* 看錯 to misread<br>*tīngcuò* 聽錯 to hear incorrectly<br>*mǎicuò* 買錯 to make a mistake in buying<br>*xiěcuò* 寫錯 to write wrongly<br>*nácuò* 拿錯 to take by mistake |
| --- | --- | --- | --- | --- |
| 11. | qīngchu | 清楚 | | clear, to be clear/distinct; used as a complement to indicate that clarity is achieved or results from an action:<br>*tīngqīngchu* 聽清楚 to listen until clarity results<br>*xiěqīngchu* 寫清楚 to write clearly |
| 12. | dǎo | 倒 | | to overturn, to spill; used as a complement to indicate that overturning, falling over or spilling results from an action:<br>*tuīdǎo* 推倒 to push/knock over<br>*dǎdǎo* 打倒 to strike down, overthrow |
| 13. | rè | 熱 | 热 | hot (temperature); to be hot |
| 14. | lěng | 冷 | | cold; to be cold |
| 15. | è | 餓 | 饿 | hungry; to be hungry |
| 16. | lèi | 累 | | to be tired |
| 17. | sǐ | 死 | | to die; used as a complement to indicate that an action is so severe that death results (often used figuratively):<br>*dǎsǐ* 打死 to beat to death<br>*rèsǐ* 熱死 to die of heat<br>*lěngsǐ* 冷死 to die of cold<br>*lèisǐ* 累死 to die of fatigue<br>*èsǐ* 餓死 to die of starvation |
| 18. | gānjing | 乾淨 | 干净 | clean |
| 19. | duì | 對 | 对 | to be correct (often used with the modal *le* to indicate the new situation which has arisen e.g. *duì le* 對了 , 'that is correct'):<br>*duìbuqǐ* 對不起 to be sorry, to have wronged someone |
| 20. | xià | 下 | | to go down; usually used as a directional complement. When used as part of a potential complement it indicates whether an object or a person can be accommodated in the space available:<br>*zuòdexià* 坐得下 able to seat<br>*zuòbuxià* 坐不下 unable to seat<br>*fàngdexià* 放得下 able to fit in<br>*fàngbuxià* 放不下 unable to fit in |

# NOTES ON GRAMMAR

## Resultative Complements

A resultative complement may be either an adjective or verb joined to a verb to indicate the result of the verb's action. Any adjective or verb may act as a complement providing the resulting combination makes sense. Once the combination is established, a close unit is formed which cannot be divided by any other element. Hence suffixes and objects are placed after the complement. The only exception to this rule is *de* 得 and its negative *bu* 不 which transforms the combination into a potential complement.

The action of the verb with a resultative complement is by definition completed, hence the negative is formed with *méi(you)* 没 (有). The negative *bu* 不 is used only when the action implies intention or is conditional e.g. 'He is unwilling to remove his things' (negative intention) is *Tā búyuànyi nákāi tāde dōngxi* 他 不 願意 拿 開 他 的 東西 and 'If you do not immediately pull him away he will beat the child to death' (negative conditional) is *Rúguǒ nǐ búlìkè lākāi tā, tā jiù huì bǎ nàge háizi dǎsǐ le* 如 果你不立刻拉開他 ， 他 就 會 把 那 個 孩子 打 死 了 .

Affirmative:
When I was in Beijing I saw many Japanese students. 我 在 北京 的 時 候 看 到 很 多 日本 學 生 。
He immediately pulled me aside. 他 立 刻 把 我 拉 開 。
I took your pencil by mistake. 我 拿 錯 了 你 的 鉛 筆 。

Negative:
I still have not found those two letters. 我 還 沒 有 找 到 那 兩 封 信 。
He has not finished writing it; teacher said that he could not go home. 他 還 沒 寫 完 ； 老 師 說 他 不 能 回 家 。
I did not use up all the money. 我 沒 把 錢 用 完 。

Interrogative:
Did you find them? 你 找 到 他 們 了 嗎 ？
Are you holding your writing brush properly? (i.e. Do you have a proper grip on your writing brush?) 你 把 毛 筆 拿 好 了 嗎 ？
Did you wash the cups clean? 你 把 杯 子 洗 乾 淨 了 沒 有 ？

## The Potential Complement

The potential may be expressed by the use of the auxiliary verb *néng* 能 e.g. 'He can tell you' is *Tā néng gàosu nǐ* 他 能 告 訴 你. However, in sentences with directional or resultative complements it is often more idiomatic to use a potential complement. The potential complement is formed by inserting *de* 得 (which retains its classical meaning of 'to be able') to express ability or *bu* 不 to express inability between the verb and the complement i.e. Verb + *de* + Complement, or Verb + *bu* + Complement. For emphasis, *néng* 能 (though redundant in English) is often used together with the potential complement.

In the affirmative, the potential complement and the complement of degree are formally indistinguishable and can be identified only by context. Thus 他 說 得 好 may mean either 'He is able to speak well' (potential) or 'He speaks/spoke well' (degree). The interrogative sentence using the particle *ma* 嗎 and containing a potential complement in the affirmative is subject to this same ambiguity, e.g. 他 說 得 好 嗎 ? may mean 'Is he able to speak well?' (potential) or 'Does/Did he speak well?' (degree). However, ambiguity of this type is limited to complements formed from adjectives. When the complement is another verb the ambiguity disappears, e.g. *zhǎodedào* 找 得 到 'able to find' and *hēdewán* 喝 得 完 'able to finish drinking' can only be potential complements.

In the negative, the potential complement and the complement of degree are quite different in form and there is no ambiguity. Compare 他 做 不 好 meaning 'He is not able to do it well' (potential) and 他 做 得 不 好 meaning 'He does/did not do it well' (degree).

As the alternative form interrogative sentence uses a negative complement there is also no ambiguity. Compare 他 做 得 好 做 不 好 ? 'Is he capable of doing it well?' (potential) and 他 做 得 好 不 好 ? meaning 'Does/Did he do it well?' (degree). In sentences where a potential complement occurs with its object, the object is placed after the complement if it is a simple object, e.g. 我 看 得 見 他 'I can see him'. Complex objects are usually transposed to the beginning of the sentence, e.g. 他 那 天 說 的 法 文 , 你 聽 得 懂 嗎 ? 'Were you able to understand the French he spoke that day?'

Affirmative:
If you go personally you will certainly be able to borrow it. 如 果 你 自 己 去 , 你 就 一 定 能 借 得 到 。
Will you be able to remember it? 你 能 記 得 住 嗎 ?
This table is heavy but I can push it aside. 這 張 桌 子 很 重 , 可 是 我 還 能 推 得 開 。
He spoke very quickly but I could still understand him. 他 說 得 很 快 , 可 是 我 還 能 聽 得 懂 。

Negative:
In the countryside one cannot buy these things. 這 些 東 西 在 鄉 下 買 不 到 。
If one does not use hot water one will not be able to wash it clean. 如 果 不 用 熱 水 洗 就 洗 不 乾 淨 。
I cannot decipher his writing. 他 寫 的 字 我 看 不 懂 。
I have written it three times but I cannot write it well. 我 寫 了 三 次 了 , 可 是 還 寫 不 好 。

Interrogative:
You have so much work to do. How can you finish doing it? 你 的 工 作 這 麼 多 , 怎 麼 能 做 得 完 ?
You have brought so much wine. How shall we be able to drink it all? 你 拿 這 麼 多 酒 來 , 我 們 怎 麼 能 喝 得 完 ?

# EXERCISES

**A.** Translate into Chinese:
1. After he learnt how to drive a car he often came to our home.
2. The water is too hot; do not give it to him.
3. If you do not go immediately they will be angry.
4. I cannot see you. Please stand up.
5. I went three times but I still could not buy it.
6. You have not washed this cup clean.
7. He remembered my name wrongly.
8. He pushed aside the old magazines.
9. He finished writing that novel last month.
10. When he speaks Japanese can you understand him?
11. He wrote my name wrongly again.
12. I am too tired at present. Please come again at five o'clock.
13. If you do not tell him then I shall.

**B.** Translate into English:

1. 你的新汽車坐得下幾個人？

2. 我的新汽車只坐得下四個人。

3. 門外邊還有幾個人，怎麼能坐得下？

4. 你的房子那麼小，住得下八個人嗎？

5. 你的汽車這麼小，我的書這麼多，怎麼放得下？

6. 我已經把那兩篇小說看了兩遍了。

7. 我今天必須把這篇小說看完。

8. 如果你不願意替我寫信，我就自己寫。

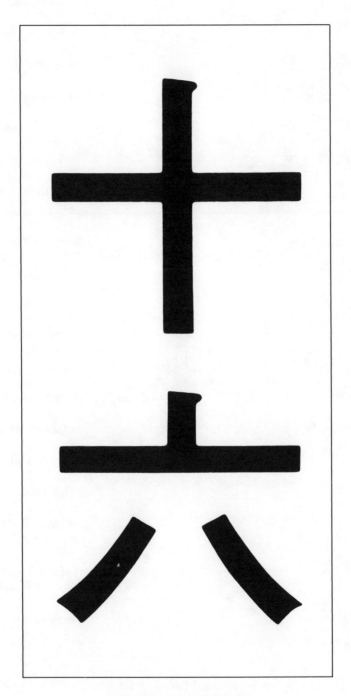

**LESSON SIXTEEN**

# VOCABULARY

| | | | | |
|---|---|---|---|---|
| 1. | diǎn(r) | 點(兒) | 点(儿) | used in expressing decimals |
| 2. | ...fēn zhī... | ...分之... | | used in expressing fractions |
| 3. | jiù | 就 | | consequently, then, soon |
| 4. | yàoshi...jiù... | 要是...就... | | if... (then)... |
| 5. | yì... jiù... | 一...就... | | as soon as... (then)... |
| 6. | zhèngxiǎng... jiù ... | 正想...就... | | just as... (then)... |
| 7. | zhèngyào... jiù... | 正要...就... | | just as... (then)... |
| 8. | cái | 才 | | only then, not until, just; formerly also written 纔 |
| 9. | xiān... zài... | 先...再... | | first... then... |
| 10. | yǐqián | 以前 | | formerly, in the past |
| 11. | yǐhòu | 以後 | 以后 | afterwards, in the future |
| 12. | ...yǐqián | ...以前 | | ...ago, before... |
| 13. | ...yǐhòu | ...以後 | ...以后 | after... |
| 14. | děng | 等 | | to wait |
| 15. | yìhuǐr | 一會兒 | 一会儿 | a (short) while |
| 16. | yíxià(r) | 一下(兒) | 一下(儿) | a (short) while |
| 17. | jiǔ | 久 | | a long time. In present day usage, there is a growing preference to use *cháng shíjiān* 長時間 (lit. 'long period of time') rather than *jiǔ* 久 |
| 18. | duō jiǔ | 多久 | | (of time) how long?; *duō cháng shíjiān* 多長時間 is also widely used |
| 19. | xiǎngqǐ | 想起 | | to think of |
| 20. | zǒu | 走 | | to leave |
| 21. | (zìcóng)... yǐlái | (自從)...以來 | (自从)...以来 | since... (a specified time) |
| 22. | ...lái | ...來 | ...来 | for the past... (specified period) |
| 23. | cóng... dào xiànzài | 從...到現在 | 从...到现在 | from... up to the present (used for short periods) |

# NOTES ON GRAMMAR

## Decimals, Fractions and Percentages

**1.** The decimal system is used extensively in China; it is the most common method of expressing parts of whole numbers. The decimal point is denoted by *diǎn* 點 e.g. 55.5 is *wǔshiwǔ diǎn wǔ* 五十五點五. Today Arabic numerals are widely used and *wǔshiwǔ diǎn wǔ* will often be written 55.5 while still retaining the Chinese reading.

**2.** Fractions are expressed in the following ways:
½ is *èr fēn zhǐ yī* 二分之一 (one out of two parts)
⅓ is *sān fēn zhǐ yī* 三分之一 (one out of three parts)
¾ is *sì fēn zhǐ sān* 四分之三 (three out of four parts)
In this construction *zhǐ* 之 is borrowed from classical Chinese and is the equivalent of *de* 的 in the modern language. *Fēn* 分 means 'part'. When fractions occur with whole numbers, the decimal system is used in Chinese, e.g. 7¾ would automatically be converted to 7.75. When an immediate conversion is not possible a translation may be made by using *yòu* 又 meaning 'and in addition', e.g. 37⅜ could be rendered *sānshiqī yòu bā fēn zhǐ sān* 三十七又八分之三.

**3.** Percentages are expressed in the following way:
20% is *bǎi fēn zhǐ èrshi* 百分之二十
95% is *bǎi fēn zhǐ jiǔshiwǔ* 百分之九十五
92.2% is *bǎi fēn zhǐ jiǔshi'èr diǎn èr* 百分之九十二點二。

## Sequence Indicators *jiù* 就, *cái* 才 and *xiān* 先 ... *zài* 再 ...

**1.** *Jiù* may be used to introduce a main clause to show that the action in the main clause is immediately consequent to that in the subordinate clause.
a) *Jiù* used to express 'then', 'consequently':
He put the book on the table and then slowly walked over (to me). 他把書放在桌子上，就慢慢地走過來。
When I heard him speak like this I became very angry.
我聽到他這樣說，就很生氣。
If you cannot go I can ask Li Wenying to go. 如果你不能去，我就可以叫李文英去。
If you do not want to drive the car, I can drive it for you. 如果你不想開車，我就可以替你開。
Often the verbal suffix *le* 了 is used with the verb of the subordinate clause to emphasize the completion of action in relation to consequent action in the main clause. The effect in this case would be like 'after Action A took place, then Action B followed':
After he did the shopping he went home. 他買了東西就回家了。
When he comes tomorrow we can ask him. 他明天來了，我們就可以問他。
I shall be able to go to the city with you when I finish writing this letter. 我把這封信寫完了，就可以跟你一起到城裏去了。
b) When *zhèngxiǎng* 正想 or *zhèngyào* 正要 occur in the subordinate clause and *jiù* meaning 'then' introduces the main clause, the idea of 'just' is conveyed:

He arrived just as I was about to go home. 我正想回家，他就來了。
He began to sing just as I was about to go to sleep. 我正要睡覺，他就開始唱歌了。
c) *Yì* 一 ...*jiù* 就... In this construction *yì* is used as an adverb meaning 'as soon as'; *jiù* meaning 'immediately' introduces the main clause and the total effect is to convey the idea of 'as soon as', e.g. *Wǒ yí kàn jiù dǒng le* 我一看就懂了 means 'I understood as soon as I had a look' or 'As soon as I had a look I understood'.
As soon as I heard him speak I knew he was French. 我一聽到他說話，就知道他是法國人了。
As soon as I think about this matter I become angry. 我一想到這件事情，就很生氣。
As soon as they told me I went to look for the teacher. 他們一告訴我，我就去找老師。
d) *Jiù* may be used as an adverb meaning 'immediately' or 'soon'. The auxiliary verb *yào* 要 and/or the modal particle *le* 了 are often used with *jiù* to indicate imminent action, e.g. *Tā jiù yào lái le* 他就要來了 'He will be here soon' or 'He will come soon'.
The train will be here soon. 火車就要來了。
I shall be finished soon. (i.e. I shall finish doing it soon.) 我就要做完了。
They will be going out soon. 他們就要出去了。

**2.** *Cái* indicates that the action of the clause in which it occurs is dependent on the action of the preceding clause. The meaning of 'only then' or 'not until' is thus expressed. Action A + *cái* + Action B means that not until Action A has happened will Action B take place.
I did not notice (see) his book until after he had left. 他走了，我才看到他的書。
He said it three times before I understood. 他說了三遍，我才聽懂。

Note that neither the suffix *le* nor the modal *le* can be used in the same clause as *cái*. *Cái* can also mean 'just' in simple sentences, e.g. *Tā cái lái* 他才來 'He just arrived'; *Tā zuótiān cái qù* 他昨天才去 'He just/only went yesterday' and *Tā cái wǔ suì* 他才五歲 'He is just five years of age'.

The choice between using *jiù* and *cái* depends largely on the attitude of the speaker, that is, the two adverbs express the modal tone of the sentence. The adverb *cái* is used when the action is delayed or does not happen promptly or when the speaker feels that the action is delayed. *Jiù* is used when the action (in the opinion of the speaker) will happen very soon; it indicates immediate consequence. Compare the following sentences:
When I heard him speak I knew that he was French. 我一聽到他說話，就知道他是法國人，
I only realized that he was French after I heard him speak. 我聽到他說話，才知道他是法國人。

**3.** *Xiān... zài...* is used when emphasis is purely on sequence of events without any implication of one action being dependent on another or that one action immediately followed another. *Xiān* meaning 'first' precedes the verb of the first clause and *zài* meaning 'then'

precedes the verb of the second clause.
I shall go to England and then France. 我先去英國，再去法國。
I shall eat first then go to your place. 我先吃了飯，再到你那兒去。

## Time Clauses Formed with *yǐqián* 以前 and *yǐhòu* 以後

**1.** *Yǐqián* and *yǐhòu* may be used as ordinary adverbs of time:
*Yǐqián* may mean 'formerly' or 'in the past' e.g. 'I did not know Chinese before' is *Wǒ yǐqián bùdǒng Zhōngwén* 我以前不懂中文。
*Yǐhòu* may mean 'afterwards' or 'in the future' e.g. 'Afterwards he did not come again' is *Yǐhòu tā méiyou zài lái* 以後他沒有再來。

**2.** *Yǐqián* and *yǐhòu* may be used to mark off time words/phrases or verbal expressions in the following ways:
a) Meaning 'ago' or 'after'/'later' respectively when used with an expression indicating a period of time:
Three years ago he was in Shanghai studying history. 三年以前他在上海學歷史。
Three weeks later he came to see me. 三個星期以後他來找我。
b) Meaning 'before' or 'after' respectively when used with a time word/phrase or verbal expresion:
Before having dinner I must finish reading this novel. 我吃飯以前要把這篇小説看完。
Prior to 1968 he was teaching English. 一九六八年以前他在教英文。
After reading this novel he began to study Japanese literature. 他看完了這篇小説以後就開始學日本文學。
It was only after he had left that I remembered his name. 他走了以後我才想起他的名字。

The following points should be observed when using *yǐqián* and *yǐhòu* with verbal expressions:
(i) Verbal expressions followed by *yǐqián* are often negated by *méi* 沒 or even *hái méi* 還沒 despite the fact that this is seemingly redundant. (Before something has happened and before something has not happened are in fact the same.) The use of *méi* and *hái méi* are for greater emphasis.
(ii) Verbal expressions followed by *yǐhòu* are often linked with the main clause by *jiù* 就, *cái* 才, or *zài* 再 showing the various types of sequence. In such cases *yǐhòu* may seem redundant. It is used to give greater emphasis.
(iii) Verbal expressions followed by *yǐqián* or *yǐhòu* refer to the time of which one is speaking and not the time at which one is speaking. Thus *yǐqián* and *yǐhòu* may refer to 'time before' or 'time after' a particular event which occurred or will occur in the past, present or future, e.g. 'We shall ask him after he arrives tomorrow' is *Tā míngtian láile yǐhòu, wǒmen jiù wèn tā* 他明天來了以後，我們就問他。

## Complements of Time Used to Indicate Duration of an Action

Complements of time are used to indicate the duration of time an action continues i.e. how long an action lasts.

**1.** Complements of time without an object to the verb:
Please wait for a while. 請你等一會兒。
I waited there for three hours. 我在那兒等了三個小時。
I watched for about half an hour before going home. 我看了半個小時才回家。

**2.** Complements of time with an object to the verb:
When the verb possesses a complement of time as well as an object the following pattern may be used:
I waited one hour for him. 我等了他一個小時。
I waited a long time before they came out. 我等了他們很長時間，他們才出來。
How long did you wait for Zhang Wenying? 你等了張文英多長時間？
Or the time phrase may be inserted between the verb and its object. Because of an inherent *de* 的, the time phrase becomes a modifier of the object, e.g. *yíge xiǎoshí (de) wénxué* 一個小時(的)文學 (one hour of literature) and as a unit follows the verb. This construction can only be used when the sense of doing certain units of time of an action is conveyed, e.g. *Tā jiāole sān nián lìshǐ* 他教了三年歷史, 'He taught history for three years'.
He studied five months of English. 他學了五個月英文。
I have studied one year of history and also two years of Japanese literature. 我學了一年歷史，還學了兩年日本文學。

**3.** Complements of time — the negative sentence:
The negative *méiyou* 沒有 is generally used when an action or state did not last for a certain period. *Méiyou* being the negative of the suffix *le* 了 will precede the verb, e.g. *Wǒ méiyou děng hěn cháng shíjiān* 我沒有等很長時間 'I did not wait a long time'. However, the use of *méiyou* with a complement of time tends to be emphatic or else expresses contradiction and 'I did not wait for long' is often translated as *Wǒ děngle bùcháng shíjiān* 我等了不長時間 i.e. 'I waited for not long'. The negative adverb *bù* 不 is used when an action or state happens/exists frequently, occurs in the present or is a supposition, e.g. 'If you do not sleep for a while you will feel too tired' is *Rúguǒ nǐ búshuì yìhuǐr, nǐ jiù huì juéde tài lèi le* 如果你不睡一會兒，你就會覺得太累了。

## Continuation of Time to the Present

**1.** Continuation of time to the present: Specified period plus *lái* 來 gives the meaning 'for the past...'; an adverb like *dōu* 都 is usually used to totalize the period.
For the past five years I have been in Nanjing. 五年來我都在南京。
He has been teaching history for the past seventeen years. 十七年來他都在教歷史。

# NOTES ON GRAMMAR

**2.** Continuation of time to the present starting from a specified point of time: (*zìcóng* 自從 /*cóng* 從 +) specified point of time + *yǐlái* 以來 gives the meaning 'since...'.

Since 1936 he has been teaching history and literature here. 自從一九三六年以來，他在這兒教歷史和文學。

Since 1977 agriculture has been flourishing in Australia. 從一九七七年以來，澳大利亞的農業很發達。

**3.** Continuation of time to the present: For short periods *lái* 來 and *yǐlái* 以來 are not used. Instead the construction *cóng* 從 ...*dào xiànzài* 到現在 is used:

Since yesterday he has been here three times. 從昨天到現在，他來過三次。

Since two o'clock he has not done any reading. 從兩點鐘到現在，他沒有看過書。

# EXERCISES

**A.** Translate into Chinese:
1. 99.5%, 5/8, 4/5, 0.067%
2. As I was about to go to sleep he asked me if I wanted to drink coffee.
3. Zhang Wenying put the things in the car and came over to talk to us.
4. When I had bought a newspaper I went to look for Zhang Wenying.
5. As soon as I found him I told him why you refused to lend him your car.
6. He will have finished eating soon, you may come in.
7. I shall first write letters and then read some novels.
8. You must tell them before telling Li Wenying.
9. They will all be going home soon.
10. Previously I did not have a house but now I have two houses.
11. In future you must first tell me.
12. After he had pushed aside the chair he slowly sat down on the floor.
13. After I told him why you were angry he began to cry.
14. They have already departed.
15. You must finish the work before you may go home.
16. After he finished writing those three novels he went to Japan.
17. Before going to Japan he wrote two letters to me.
18. I have already waited two hours, I cannot wait any longer.
19. How long have you been waiting for them?
20. I listened for half an hour before going home.
21. We all studied two years of Chinese history.
22. For the past two months he has been in France.
23. Since January they have been studying English literature.
24. From this morning I have been studying French history.

**B.** Translate into English:
1. 我正想吃飯，他就來找我了。
2. 我一看到他，就告訴他你已經走了。
3. 我等了半個小時才回家。
4. 我等了一個小時，他才打電話來告訴我他不回家了。
5. 我在北京住了三年。
6. 你們在廣州住了多長時間？
7. 你走了以後，他就回上海去了。
8. 我教了八年中文，現在不想再教了。
9. 九年來他們都在這兒學習日本文學。
10. 一九六六年以來，他去過中國六次。
11. 對不起，你在這兒等了多長時間了？
12. 他要把工作做完才可以回家。
13. 叫他們先把手洗乾淨再進來吃飯。
14. 那個學生才十五歲。

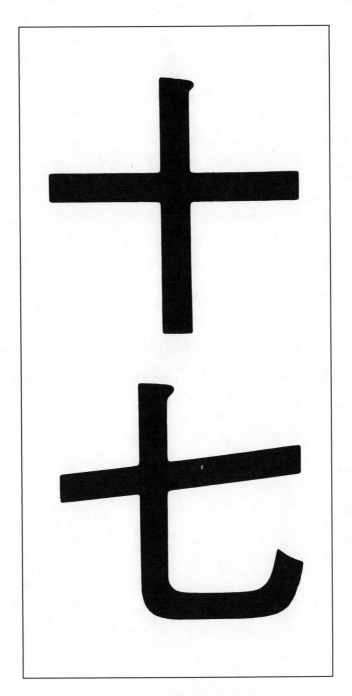

**LESSON SEVENTEEN**

# VOCABULARY

| | | | |
|---|---|---|---|
| 1. měi | 每 | | each, every |
| 2. shì | 試 | 试 | to try |
| 3. kěn | 肯 | | to be willing to |
| 4. jì | 寄 | | to send by post |
| 5. kǎolù | 考慮 | 考虑 | to consider (i.e. to turn over in one's mind) |
| 6. huài | 壞 | 坏 | bad |
| 7. huài le | 壞了 | 坏了 | to be spoiled (of food); to be out of order, to have broken down |
| 8. wénzhāng | 文章 | | essay; journal or newspaper article (cl. 篇) |
| 9. bànfa | 辦法 | 办法 | way, means (of dealing with a matter) |
| 10. yǒu bànfa | 有辦法 | 有办法 | to have the means (of dealing with a matter) |
| 11. méi(yǒu) bànfa | 沒(有)辦法 | 沒(有)办法 | unable to deal/cope (with) |
| 12. guānxi | 關係 | 关系 | relationship, consequence |
| 13. méi(yǒu) guānxi | 沒(有)關係 | 沒(有)关系 | of no consequence, does not matter |
| 14. fāngbiàn | 方便 | | convenient |
| 15. cháng | 嘗 | 尝 | to taste |
| 16. duō | 多 | | more, many |
| 17. shǎo | 少 | | few, less |
| 18. gěi | 給 | 给 | to let (i.e. to give a person a chance to do something), used as a complement meaning 'to (someone)' |
| 19. zài | 在 | | used as a complement meaning 'in', 'on' |
| 20. dào | 到 | | used as a complement meaning 'to (place)' or 'until (time/state)' |
| 21. chéng | 成 | | used as a complement meaning '(make/turn) into' or '(to treat) as' |
| 22. fānyi | 翻譯 | 翻译 | to translate |
| 23. fānyichéng | 翻譯成 | 翻译成 | to translate into |

# VOCABULARY

| | | | | |
|---|---|---|---|---|
| 24. | bāngzhù | 幫助 | 帮助 | to help. *Bāngmáng* 幫忙 is more commonly used in spoken Chinese for 'to help', having the literal meaning of 'to help one in what one is busy doing'. *Bāngmáng*, however, cannot be used with an object or complement as *máng* (busy) is the object of *bāng*. |
| 25. | bāngbangmáng | 幫幫忙 | 帮帮忙 | to help out; 'to give a hand' (also *bāng ge máng* 幫個忙 ) |

# NOTES ON GRAMMAR

## Each and Every

There is a limited number of idiomatic expressions in which the noun is reduplicated, e.g. *shān shān yǒu hǔ* 山山有虎, 'There is a tiger on every mountain'; *shì shì rú yì* 事事如意, 'May everything be as you would have it'.

Most classifiers may be reduplicated: *tiān tiān* 天天 'each/every day'; *nián nián* 年年 'each/every year'; *gè gè xuésheng* 個個學生 'each/every student' etc. The adverb *dōu* 都 may be used for emphasis, e.g. 'He goes every day' is *Tā tiān tiān dōu qù* 他天天都去.
The adjective *měi* 每 may be used with any noun to give the meaning 'each'. Usually a classifier will stand between *měi* and the noun it qualifies e.g. *měige xuésheng* 每個學生 is 'each student'. However, those nouns which normally do not use classifiers because they are in a sense themselves classifiers will of course stand immediately after *měi* without a classifier, e.g. *měinián* 每年 is 'each year', *měitiān* 每天 is 'each day' and *měicì* 每次 is 'each time'. The adverb *dōu* 都 is usually used before the predicate of a subject qualified by 'each' whether it be a noun qualified by *měi* or a reduplicated noun or classifier. The adverb *dōu* emphasizes that there is no exception and the whole construction may be translated as 'every'.
Each year he helps me many times. 他每年都幫助我很多次。
Everyone understands. 人人都懂。
Every student should consider this matter. 每個學生都應該考慮這個問題。
Every character was written wrongly. 每個字都寫錯了。

## The Reduplication of Verbs

Some verbs may be reduplicated to express short, quick, informal or random action, action repeated over and over again and action denoting trial or attempt. The reduplicated section is pronounced in the neutral tone; in the case of disyllabic verbs only the first syllable of the reduplicated verb is stressed, e.g. *kànkan* 看看 'to have a look' and *kǎolükaolü* 考慮考慮 'to give a matter some thought'.

Please have a look. 請你看看。
He does not understand; please say it again for him. 他不懂；請你再給他説説。
I shall introduce you to each other. 我給你們介紹介紹。
This type of fruit is very good. Have a try. 這種水果很好，你嘗嘗。

An effect similar to the reduplication of the verb may be achieved in the following ways:
**1.** Monosyllabic verbs may take the complement *yi* 一 + the same verb.
I would like to have a look at the essay you wrote this morning. 我想看一看你今天早上寫的文章。
Please wait for a while. 請你等一等。
**2.** Monosyllabic or disyllabic verbs may take the complement *yíxià* 一下.
We shall have to give some consideration to the matter. 這個問題，我們要考慮一下。
This (particular type of) wine is excellent. Please try it. 這種酒非常好，請你嘗一下。
**3.** The verbal suffix *le* may be used with monosyllabic verbs which have been reduplicated. When used it is placed between the two verbs.
He spoke for a while about past events and then went home to sleep. 他説了説以前的事情，就回家睡覺去了。
He had a look and told me that he did not want to buy it. 他看了看就告訴我他不想買了。

## *Zài* 在, *gěi* 給, *dào* 到 and *chéng* 成 Used as Resultative Complements

**1.** *Zài* shows that someone/something is in or at a certain place as a result of a particular action. This use of *zài* is only possible with a limited number of verbs and a place word must follow.
He was seated at the back. 他坐在後邊。
He is living in the country. 他住在鄉下。
In 1975 he was still living in Shanghai. 一九七五年他還住在上海。
He wrote his name on my book. 他把他的名字寫在我的書上。

**2.** *Gěi* links the verb with its indirect object; the indirect object must be used although the direct object may be omitted if it is clear from the context. *Gěi* may be translated as 'to (someone)'.

The letter he wrote me was extremely long. 他寫給我的信非常長。

The fruit you sold me this morning has already gone bad. 你今天早上賣給我的水果已經壞了。

He sent me (by post) many things last year. 去年他寄給我很多東西。

Please introduce your friend to us. 請你把你的朋友介紹給我們。

**3.** *Dào* followed by a place word means 'to'. When it is followed by a time word or a state it means 'until'.

We read until three o'clock and then went home. 我們看到三點鐘，就回家去了。

He sent the letter to Beijing but I had already left. 他把那封信寄到北京，可是我已經走了。

**4.** *Chéng* has a basic meaning of 'to accomplish', 'to be successful'. It may be used as a complement indicating successful completion of an action with certain types of verbs and may be translated as '(to treat/regard) as' or '(to make/convert) into'.

I want to translate this novel into French. 我想把這篇小說翻譯成法文。

He regards me as a fifteen year old child. 他把我看成一個十五歲的孩子。

He wants me to help him translate this article into Chinese but I am too busy. 他要我幫助他把這篇文章翻譯成中文，可是我太忙了。

## The Indefinite Use of Interrogative Words

**1.** Most interrogative words may be used to convey the indefinite idea of 'any' (person, place, amount, thing, manner) or every member of a category. The interrogative word is stressed and followed by *dōu* 都 or *yě* 也 before the verb. When the verb is negated the sense is 'no-one', 'nowhere', 'no amount', 'nothing', 'not any', 'no matter how' etc. The use of *shénme* 什麼 and *shéi/shuí* 誰 in this way is common but the use of other interrogative words is limited and less common.

He has everything. 他什麼都有。

He has every type of book. 他什麼書都有。

He is incapable of doing anything well. 他什麼事都做不好。

Everyone likes him. 誰都喜歡他。

No-one was willing to help. 誰都不願意幫忙。

Nowhere are things as cheap as they are here. 哪兒的東西都沒有這兒的便宜。

In no year were things as expensive as they are now. 哪年的東西都沒有現在的貴。

However he said it he was unable to say it clearly. 他怎麼說都說不清楚。

However he wrote it he was unable to write it well. 他怎麼寫都寫不好。

No amount of money will be able to buy it. 多少錢都買不到。

Any amount of money will do. 多少錢都行。

You may purchase any number. 你買多少都可以。

You may give me any number (up to 10) of pencils. 你給我幾枝鉛筆都可以。

It does not matter how long I wait for you. 我等你多長時間都沒關係。

It does not matter how far away you live. I have my own car. 你住多遠都沒關係，我自己有汽車。

**2.** Interrogative words may also be used to convey the indefinite meaning of 'some place', 'some person', 'some amount' etc. which cannot be specified or which one does not wish or feel the need to specify, or the indefinite meaning of moderation in negative sentences e.g. 'not so', 'not very', 'not particularly'. In both of these cases the word order is the same as for an interrogative sentence. However used with an indefinite meaning the interrogative word is not stressed i.e. it is pronounced in the neutral tone whereas used as an interrogative word it is stressed, e.g.

*Tā xiǎng chī diǎnr shénme?* 他想吃點兒什麼? means 'What does he want to eat (a little of)?'
whereas
*Tā xiǎng chī diǎnr shenme* 他想吃點兒什麼 means 'He wants to eat a little of something.'

Apart from the stress or lack of stress in pronunciation often the context as well as other elements in the sentence itself will clarify the meaning. An interrogative word may have an indefinite meaning in a sentence while another interrogative word or interrogative clause serves to form the question.

'some place', 'some person', 'some amount':
How about it if we go somewhere to buy some fruit? 我們去哪兒買點兒水果，好不好？
The car has broken down. How about it if we find someone to help us? 汽車壞了，找誰來幫忙，好不好？

'not so', 'not very', 'not particularly':
His new house is not particularly good. 他的新房子不怎麼好。
This novel is not particularly well-written. 這篇小說寫得不怎麼好。

**3.** Interrogative words may be used in an indefinite sense to convey the meaning of 'whichever one', 'whatever', 'however much' etc. In this case the interrogative word is used in the subordinate clause and repeated in the main clause. Usually the repeated interrogative word is preceded by the sequence indicator *jiù* 就. The construction is balanced and the effect is emphatic.

He did whatever came to his mind. 他想到什麼就做什麼。
I shall use however much you give me. 你給我多少，我就用多少。
I shall go wherever you go. 你去哪兒，我就去哪兒。

# EXERCISES

**A.** Translate into Chinese:
1. We shall come whenever it is convenient for you.
2. I shall buy whatever you buy.
3. We did whatever the teacher told us to do.
4. He is not particularly good at driving a car.
5. You may put those old magazines anywhere.
6. However much you buy does not matter.
7. The place where I am staying is very inconvenient. It is too far from the school.
8. Please have a try.
9. No-one can understand the Japanese he speaks.
10. He goes to Nanjing each year.
11. Please wait for a while, they will come soon.
12. He had a look and then slowly walked over (to me).
13. I want to introduce Zhang Wenying to him.
14. He takes the children to school and then goes to work.
15. Teacher asked me to translate these two essays into French.
16. They live in Guangzhou.
17. Please sit at the front.
18. Do not treat me like a child.
19. No-one dares to help him.
20. No-one is willing to do it for him.

**B.** Translate into English:

1. 他告訴我這個新方法很好，我想試試。
2. 他怎麼都不肯告訴我。
3. 我要先考慮一下。
4. 我的汽車壞了。我要找李文英，他一定有辦法。
5. 你應該少喝點兒酒，多喝點兒牛奶。
6. 他們站在門外面說話。
7. 我現在住在城裏，買東西很方便。
8. 他先把我送到上海，自己再坐船回到廣州去。
9. 你喝什麼，我就喝什麼。
10. 把中文翻譯成英文不容易，可是把英文翻譯成中文更不容易。
11. 請你再等一等，他們就要來了。
12. 我沒有辦法替你把這篇文章翻譯成中文。

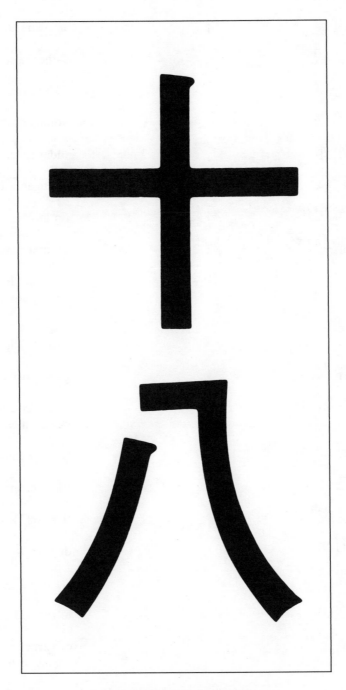

**LESSON EIGHTEEN**

# VOCABULARY

| | | | | |
|---|---|---|---|---|
| 1. | děi | 得 | | must |
| 2. | qīnqi | 親戚 | 亲戚 | relative |
| 3. | mǔqin | 母親 | 母亲 | mother; also *māma* 媽媽 |
| 4. | fùqin | 父親 | 父亲 | father; also *bàba* 爸爸 |
| 5. | gēge | 哥哥 | | older brother |
| 6. | dìdi | 弟弟 | | younger brother |
| 7. | jiějie | 姐姐 | | older sister |
| 8. | mèimei | 妹妹 | | younger sister |
| 9. | kànqilai | 看起來 | 看起来 | on looking at, in appearance |
| 10. | zuòqilai | 做起來 | 做起来 | on doing, to begin to do |
| 11. | bìng | 並 | 并 | negative intensifier giving the sense 'not by any means' (used with 不 or 沒) |
| 12. | háo | 毫 | | negative intensifier giving the sense 'not the slightest' (used with 不 or 沒) |
| 13. | kèren | 客人 | | guest, visitor |
| 14. | kèqi | 客氣 | 客气 | polite, courteous, to act like a guest; to stand on ceremony |
| 15. | lián | 連 | 连 | used in emphatic constructions |
| 16. | shi | 是 | | used for emphasizing the affirmative |
| 17. | láohu | 老虎 | | tiger (cl. 隻 ) |
| 18. | gǒu | 狗 | | dog (cl. 隻 , 條 ) |
| 19. | māo | 貓 | 猫 | cat (cl. 隻 ) |
| 20. | pǎochu | 跑出 | | to run out (from somewhere) |
| 21. | shi... de | 是...的 | | construction stressing time, place, means or the agent of an action |

# NOTES ON GRAMMAR

## Emphasis

The position of a word in an earlier part of a sentence gives it definite reference and also greater emphasis in relation to other words of the sentence. Therefore the object of a sentence is emphasized by transposing it to a position in front of or immediately following the subject. Previous lessons have shown the use of the pretransitive *bǎ* 把 construction and the use of *yě* 也 and *dōu* 都 following an interrogative adjective plus the object; both these constructions transpose the object to emphasize it. The following are other common constructions used for achieving emphasis.

**1.** Simple transposing of the object:

It is possible to emphasize the object simply by transposing it either to a position at the front of the sentence or immediately after the subject.

OBJECT (+ SUBJECT + ADVERB) + VERB (+ INDIRECT OBJECT)

I must finish writing this essay this evening. 這篇文章我今天晚上一定要寫完。

(SUBJECT +) OBJECT (+ ADVERB) + VERB (+ INDIRECT OBJECT)

Before he had finished eating his meal he angrily left. 他飯還沒吃完，就生氣地走了。

**2.** The rhetorical question:

The negative question may be used for emphasis of the affirmative, e.g. *Tā shi Zhōngguorén* 他是中國人 (He is Chinese) is given emphasis by the rhetorical question *Tā búshi Zhōngguorén ma* 他不是中國人嗎? (Is he not Chinese?)

Is this not yours? 這不是你的嗎？
Are you not going? 你不去嗎？
Won't you buy it? 你不買嗎？

**3.** The double negative:

A strong affirmative may be achieved by the use of two negatives in the following ways:

a) A negative verb followed by a further negative which modifies an expression of sanction, e.g. *bù...bùxíng* 不...不行:

You must buy some. 你不買一些不行。
You must go. 你不去不行。
You must buy those two books. 你不買那兩本書不行。

b) A negative occurring in each of the two clauses linked with *jiù* 就. In each of these sentences the modal particle *le* 了 may be used to emphasize the new situation which has arisen:

Without his help I would have no means of coping by myself. 如果他不幫忙，我自己就沒辦法了。

Without his sending money to me I would not be able to cope. 如果他不寄錢給我，我就沒辦法了。

**4.** Emphatic negation may be achieved in the following ways:

a) *Yì* 一 + CLASSIFIER + NOUN + *dōu* 都 /*yě* 也 + NEGATIVE ADVERB + VERB

In this construction the numeral 'one' gives the total effect of 'not even one' or 'not even a'.

I do not have even one dollar. 我一塊錢都沒有。
I cannot lend you even one dollar. 我一塊錢都不能借給你。
We do not even have a chair. 我們一把椅子也沒有。

b) *Yìdiǎnr* 一點兒 + NOUN + *dōu* 都 /*yě* 也 + NEGATIVE ADVERB + VERB

I do not understand even a little Chinese. 我一點兒中文也不懂。
He cannot speak even a little Japanese. 他一點兒日語都不會說。

c) By the use of negative intensifiers such as *bìng* 並 and *háo* 毫:

He is not by any means as tall as my father. 他並沒有我爸爸那麼高。
Without the slightest reservation, he told me that my novel was written badly. 他毫不客氣地告訴我,我的小說寫得不好。

**5.** The (*lián* 連)... *dōu* 都 /*yě* 也 construction may be used to emphasize the subject, object or verb of a sentence. The use of *lián* is optional in most cases while *dōu* or *yě* of this construction is the essential element.

a) Emphasizing the subject: (*lián*) + SUBJECT + *dōu*/*yě* + VERB + OBJECT

Even a child knows how to do it. How is it that you do not? 連孩子都會,你怎麼不會？
Even he wants to go. 連他也想去。

b) Emphasizing the object: SUBJECT (+ *lián*) + OBJECT + *dōu*/*yě* + VERB

He was unwilling to see even his father. 他連父親也不肯見。
He refuses to drink even water. 他連水都不願意喝。

or

(*lián* +) OBJECT + SUBJECT + *dōu*/*yě* + VERB

In 1936 he sold even (his) bed. 一九三六年連床他都賣了。

c) Emphasizing the verb:

SUBJECT (+ *lián*) + VERB + *dōu*/*yě* + NEGATIVE ADVERB + AUXILIARY VERB (+ VERB)

or

SUBJECT (+ *lián*) + VERB + *dōu*/*yě* + NEGATIVE ADVERB + VERB + OTHER ELEMENT

In this construction note the following:

i      The verb must be repeated after *dōu* or *yě*.
ii     Generally this construction is used with a negative adverb and/or an auxiliary verb; these stand before the repeated verb.
iii    When an auxiliary verb is used, the repeated verb may be omitted.

iv    Often a complement will follow the repeated verb when an auxiliary verb is not used.

v    If there is an object, it generally stands before the subject.

He would not even look at it. 他連看都不肯看一下。

He was not willing to even try. 他連試都不肯試一下。

I cannot even read his writing. 他寫的字我連看都看不懂。

**6.** The use of *shi* 是 to express assertion:

a) *Shi* may be used to give emphasis to verbs and adjectival predicates by expressing assertion with the sense 'it is true that' or 'it is the case that'.

He does live in Nanjing. 他是住在南京。

Chinese do write with brushes. 中國人是用毛筆寫字。

b) *Shi* may also be used to give a contrast between verbs and between adjectival predicates.

This thing is heavy, not big. 這件東西是重，不是大。

I am telling you not asking you. 我是告訴你，不是問你。

I want to buy fish not fruit. 我是想買魚，不是想買水果。

**7.** The use of *jiù* 就 to emphasize the assertive *shi* 是 : *Jiùshi* has the meaning of 'nothing but', 'simply', 'just'.

He simply likes drinking wine. 他就是喜歡喝酒。

I just do not like him. 我就是不喜歡他。

**8.** The subject of a subject + verb + object sentence or a sentence with an adjectival predicate may be stressed by converting such sentences into sentences with equational constructions, e.g. in the subject + verb + object sentence 'He sells fish' (*Tā mài yú* 他賣魚 ), the subject 'he' may be stressed by rendering 'sells fish' (*mài yú* 賣魚 ) into the nominal expression 'one who sells fish' (*mài yú de* 賣魚的 ) and equating the subject and nominal expression with the verb *shi*, i.e. *Tā shi mài yú de* 他是賣魚的. Similarly, in the subject + *hěn* + adjectival predicate sentence 'This house is old' (*Zhèsuǒ fángzi hěn jiù* 這所房子很舊 ) stress may be placed on 'this house' (*zhèsuǒ fángzi* 這所房子 ) by converting the adjectival predicate 'is old' (*hěn jiù* 很舊 ) into 'an old one' or 'one which is old' (*jiù de* 舊的) and equating the subject and the nominal expression with the verb *shi*, i.e. *Zhèsuǒ fángzi shi jiù de* 這所房子是舊的。

**9.** The *shi... de* construction is used to stress the circumstances (time, place, means or agent) of a completed action. This construction gives an explanatory tone to the sentence and hence places emphasis on the circumstances of the action and gives the sense 'it was on/at/by ... that an action took place'. In the construction *shi* may be omitted in affirmative sentences. However, in negative sentences *shi* must be retained and linked with the negative adverb *bù*.

Emphasizing the time: I arrived yesterday. 我是昨天來的。

Emphasizing the means: He came by plane. 他是坐飛機來的。

Emphasizing the place: He comes from China. 他是從中國來的。

Emphasizing the agent: I wrote this essay. (lit. 'It was I who wrote this essay.') 這是我寫的文章 or 這篇文章是我寫的。

The negative form of this construction also refers to completed action; it refers to action not having been completed at a certain time, in a certain place or in a certain manner.

He did not come by train. 他不是坐火車來的。

I did not arrive yesterday. 我不是昨天來的。

He did not come from China. 他不是從中國來的。

**10.** Emphasis on appearance, disappearance and state of existence of things with indefinite reference is achieved by changing the word order:

a) Verbs of action followed by *zhe* 着 emphasize state of existence.

Some books were lying on the table. 桌子上放着一些書。

A few students were still standing outside. 外邊還站着幾個學生。

Several guests were seated inside. 裏邊坐着幾個客人。

b) Verbs of arrival or departure followed by the suffix *le* 了 or any verb with its complement emphasize appearance or disappearance.

A guest just arrived. 剛才來了一個客人。

Yesterday three tigers escaped. 昨天跑了三隻老虎。

# EXERCISES

**A.** Translate into Chinese:
1. Even my younger sister can drive a car.
2. He refuses to even take a look.
3. This bag is heavy, I cannot budge it.
4. His father sells books.
5. My mother teaches there.
6. I have few relatives here.
7. Even Zhang Wenying refuses to go.
8. When you start to do it, it is not at all difficult.
9. Those three students come from Shanghai.
10. Just as I was about to go to sleep two guests arrived.
11. Some people were standing outside.
12. They would not even listen.

**B.** Translate into English:
1. 椅子上放着一些舊書。
2. 床上躺着一個老人。
3. 學校前邊還站着三四個學生。
4. 從樓上走下來幾個客人。
5. 房子外邊躺着三隻黑狗。
6. 我是想喝酒，不是想喝水。
7. 裏邊坐着幾個客人。
8. 我是前年來的，你呢？
9. 我今年六月份來的。
10. 那三個學生是坐火車來的。
11. 他連我都不肯告訴，
12. 他並不比我高。
13. 他毫不客氣地告訴我，我用了他的杯子。
14. 做起來，這種工作並不怎麼難。
15. 他是我的親戚，不是我的朋友。
16. 看起來，你並沒有我哥哥高。
17. 你們不要客氣吧！喜歡喝什麼就喝什麼。

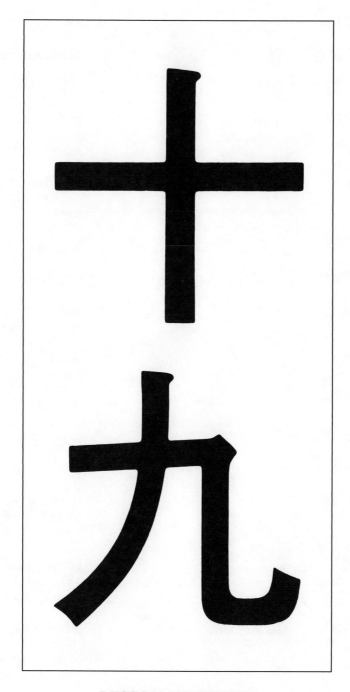

**LESSON NINETEEN**

# VOCABULARY

| | | | |
|---|---|---|---|
| 1. ne | 呢 | | modal particle |
| 2. ba | 吧 | | modal particle |
| 3. zāng | 髒 | 脏 | dirty |
| 4. nòng | 弄 | | to make, to do, to manipulate |
| 5. nòngzāng | 弄髒 | 弄脏 | to soil, to make dirty |
| 6. nònghuài | 弄壞 | 弄坏 | to put out of order, to ruin |
| 7. chuān | 穿 | | to wear |
| 8. shuāng | 雙 | 双 | a pair (classifier for things measured in sets of two, e.g. shoes, socks, chopsticks) |
| 9. yīfu | 衣服 | | clothing (cl. 件 ) |
| 10. kùzi | 褲子 | 裤子 | trousers (cl. 條 ) |
| 11. wàzi | 襪子 | 袜子 | sock (cl. 隻 e.g. two socks, 兩隻襪子 but a pair of socks, 一雙襪子 ) |
| 12. xié | 鞋 | | shoe (cl. 隻 e.g. two shoes, 兩隻鞋 but a pair of shoes, 一雙鞋 ) |
| 13. qúnzi | 裙子 | | skirt (cl. 條 ) |
| 14. chīguāng | 吃光 | | to eat all of; to eat up completely |
| 15. yòngguāng | 用光 | | to use all of; to use up completely |
| 16. kuàizi | 筷子 | | chopstick (cl. *gēn* 根, e.g. two chopsticks 兩根筷子 , but a pair of chopsticks 一雙筷子 ) |
| 17. wǎn | 碗 | | bowl (cl. 個 e.g. one rice bowl 一個飯碗); bowl of, e.g. one bowl of rice 一碗飯, a big bowl of rice 一大碗飯 |
| 18. pánzi | 盤子 | 盘子 | plate (cl. 個, e.g. a plate 一個盤子 ) |
| 19. pán | 盤 | 盘 | plate of, plateful e.g. three plates of fruit 三盤水果 |
| 20. shūcài | 蔬菜 | | green vegetables |
| 21. miàntiáo | 麵條 | 面条 | noodles |
| 22. ròu | 肉 | | meat |
| 23. zhūròu | 豬肉 | | pork (*zhū* 豬, pig) |
| 24. yángròu | 羊肉 | | mutton (*yáng* 羊, sheep) |
| 25. niúròu | 牛肉 | | beef (*niú* 牛, cattle) |
| 26. bèi | 被 | | indicator of the passive |

# VOCABULARY

| | | | | |
|---|---|---|---|---|
| 27. | jiào | 叫 | | indicator of the passive |
| 28. | gěi | 給 | 给 | indicator of the passive |
| 29. | ràng | 讓 | 让 | indicator of the passive |
| 30. | shòu | 受 | | indicator of the passive |
| 31. | názǒu | 拿走 | | take away |

# NOTES ON GRAMMAR

## The Modal Particles *ne* 呢 and *ba* 吧

A modal particle is used to indicate the mood of the clause or sentence at the end of which it stands. Modal particles are pronounced in the neutral tone.

**1.** The modal particle *ba* may be used at the end of a narrative sentence to express

a) Uncertainty, doubt or probability:

You don't know do you?; You wouldn't know, I suppose. 你不知道吧?

I suppose you have been to China; You have been to China, haven't you? 你去過中國吧?

He is not going, is he?; I suppose he is not going. 他不去吧?

You are hungry, aren't you?; I guess you are hungry. 你餓了吧?

b) Suggestion or mild command:

Sit down!; Take a seat! 坐吧!

Let's go (i.e. leave)! 走吧!

Let's eat! 吃飯吧!

c) Agreement:

All right!; Okay! 好吧!

All right!, sell it! 好,把它賣了吧!

**2.** The modal particle *ne* is used in the following ways:

a) As a particle expressing doubt used at the end of interrogative sentences:

And will you be going? 你去不去呢?

Who can he be looking for? 他找誰呢?

b) As an interrogative particle forming a question in a known or stated context:

He sings well, what about you? 他歌唱得很好,你呢?

He likes travelling by plane, do you? 他喜歡坐飛機,你呢?

We want to go today, what about you? 我們想今天去,你呢?

How about Mr Zhang?; Where is Mr Zhang? 張先生呢?

c) As a particle indicating a continuing action. (See Lesson Ten)

## The Passive Voice

In the Chinese language, extensive use of a topical subject (transposed object) makes the use of the passive form less important than in English. It is easier to define the subject and predicate in a Chinese sentence as 'topic and comment' rather than 'actor and action' and to include the second definition in the first. Thus the sentence *Mǐ yòu yòngwán le* 米又用完了 in which *mǐ* is the topical subject would be translated into English with the verb in the passive, i.e. 'The rice is used up again'. Note that a sentence with a topical subject (which in English becomes the grammatical subject with a verb in the passive voice) generally contains a complement, e.g. 'He speaks Japanese well' 他的日語說得很好. (See Lesson Eight) The *shi... de* construction may also be used to transform a subject + verb + object sentence into a sentence in the passive voice by transposing the object, i.e. object + *shi* (+ subject) + verb + *de*, e.g. 'This book was purchased by him' 這本書是他買的. (See Lesson Eighteen)

The passive indicators *bèi* 被, *ràng* 讓, *gěi* 給, *jiào* 叫 and *shòu* 受 emphasize an action and its result and make the passive voice explicit; *shòu* meaning 'to receive' can be linked with a few nouns to translate the passive voice. In written Chinese *bèi* is commonly used while in speech *ràng*, *jiào* and *gěi* are preferred. These words are now often classed as prepositions and their use follows the ordinary prepositional construction. When the agent is unknown, *rén* 人 (unspecified person/persons) may be used. In the case of *bèi* the agent may be omitted and *bèi* may be followed directly by a verb. However, it is not possible to omit the agent in the case of other passive indicators.

SUBJECT + PASSIVE INDICATOR + AGENT + VERB + OTHER ELEMENTS

a) The use of *bèi* without an agent:

The clothes I washed have been soiled. 我洗的衣服被弄髒了。

The wine he brought has all been drunk. 他拿來的酒都被喝光了。

# NOTES ON GRAMMAR

b) The use of passive indicators (*bèi, jiào, gěi, ràng*) with an agent:

The bowls have all been washed clean by Zhang Wenying. 那些碗都給張文英洗乾淨了。

The book which the teacher lent me has been soiled by that child. 老師借給我的書叫那個孩子弄髒了。

My watch has been ruined by you. 我的手錶讓你弄壞了。

The beef has all been eaten up by them. 牛肉都被他們吃光了。

c) The use of *shòu* with a limited number of nouns to convey the passive voice:

He was influenced by this type of thinking. 他受了這種思想的影響。

His work was also affected by this sort of thinking. 他的工作也受了這種思想的影響。

---

# EXERCISES

**A.** Translate into Chinese:

1. That child has ruined my watch (by fiddling around with it).
2. We were all influenced by this type of thinking.
3. He is not likely to go, is he?
4. The skirt you lent me has been soiled.
5. I do not like wearing stockings.
6. Let's go to look for Zhang Wenying.
7. He does not eat green vegetables. He only eats meat.
8. Pork is not as expensive as beef.
9. Do you know how to use chopsticks?
10. The ricebowls and chopsticks have all been put on the table.
11. This dish is too big. Give me a small one.
12. What would you like to eat. Noodles or rice?
13. The noodles have all been eaten up by the children.
14. My skirt is too long.
15. These socks are dirty.
16. I want to purchase two ricebowls.
17. These shoes are very heavy.
18. I want to buy some pork and some mutton.
19. He drinks a lot of wine. He drank up all the wine I just bought.
20. He is still getting dressed. Please wait a while.

**B.** Translate into English:

1. 我很早已經穿好衣服在這裏等他。
2. 妹妹把新衣服弄髒了。
3. 這條褲子太長。
4. 那兩條裙子太貴。
5. 這個孩子把一大碗麵條吃完了。
6. 我剛才買的蔬菜被他用光了。
7. 牛肉昨天用光了，今天要再買一點兒。
8. 這兒一點兒肉都沒有了。
9. 我還想吃一點兒蔬菜。
10. 筷子、飯碗都放在桌子上。
11. 你用錯了筷子，這雙是我的。
12. 我的手錶給你弄壞了。
13. 你穿的裙子跟我的一樣舊。
14. 這個月蔬菜跟肉都很貴。
15. 杯子跟盤子給誰拿走了？
16. 請你們等一會兒，他還沒有穿好衣服呢！
17. 他們是三天以前來的。
18. 這種飯碗很貴吧？
19. 我的衣服弄髒了，我洗了半個小時，可是還洗不乾淨。

**LESSON TWENTY**

# VOCABULARY

| | | | |
|---|---|---|---|
| 1. duì(zhe) | 對（着） | 对（着） | facing, towards, to |
| 2. duì(yu) | 對（於） | 对（于） | in regard to, for, towards |
| 3. guānyu | 關於 | 关于 | concerning, regarding, about |
| 4. yǒu qù | 有趣 | | to be interesting |
| 5. duì... gǎn xìngqu | 對...感興趣 | 对...感兴趣 | to be interested in...; *duì...bùgǎn xìng-qu* 對...不感興趣 not interested in... |
| 6. tàidu | 態度 | 态度 | attitude |
| 7. lai/qu | 來，去 | 来，去 | to (in order to) |
| 8. yòu... yòu... | 又...又... | | both... and... |
| 9. chúle... (yǐwài) | 除了...（以外） | | besides, in addition to, as well as, apart from |
| 10. búdàn... érqiě... | 不但...而且... | | not only... but also... |
| 11. yuè... yuè... | 越...越... | | the more... the more... |
| 12. yuè lai yuè... | 越來越... | 越来越... | increasingly... |
| 13. bù... bù... | 不...不... | | (if) not... not... ; not... unless... |
| 14. yìbiānr... yìbiānr... | 一邊兒...一邊兒... | 一边儿...一边儿... | (doing one thing) while at the same time (doing something else) |
| 15. jìrán... jiù... | 既然...就... | | since... then... |
| 16. jiǎrú... jiù... | 假如...就... | | if... then... |
| 17. chúfēi... yàoburán... | 除非...要不然... | | not... unless... |
| 18. chúfēi... cái... | 除非...才... | | only if... will then... |
| 19. búshi... jiùshi... | 不是...就是... | | if not... then... |
| 20. zhǐyào... jiù... | 只要...就... | | provided that; so long as... then... |
| 21. jì... yòu... | 既...又... | | both... and... |
| 22. suīrán... yě... | 雖然...也... | 虽然...也... | although... yet... |
| 23. yǐnwei... suóyi... | 因爲...所以... | 因为...所以... | because... therefore... |
| 24. zhèng yǐnwei... suóyi... | 正因爲...所以... | 正因为...所以... | it is precisely because... that... |
| 25. jiùshi... yě... | 就是...也... | | even if... still... |
| 26. gāng... jiù... | 剛...就... | 刚...就... | just as... then... |
| 27. bùguǎn... yě... | 不管...也... | | no matter... still... |

# NOTES ON GRAMMAR

## The Prepositions *duì(zhe)* 對 ( 着 ), *duì(yu)* 對 ( 於 ) **and** *guānyu* 關 於

**1.** *Duì(zhe)* means 'facing', 'towards', 'to', e.g. *Tā duì xuésheng shuō zhège fāngfa bùhǎo* 他對學生説這個方法不好. (He said to the students that this method is not good.) Note that in a sentence using *duìzhe* and the verb *shuō* 説 i.e. A *duìzhe* B *shuō* usually there is the implication that A is facing B while speaking.

He slowly said to us, 'Don't let him find out about this matter!' 他慢慢地對我們説,'這件事情不能讓他知道.'

He often speaks to us like that. 他常常這樣對我們説話 。

**2.** *Duì(yu)* may be used to modify either a noun, pronoun or verb to give the meaning 'in regard to'. Note however, that *duì(yu)* cannot be used after auxiliary verbs or adverbs.

I am not interested in politics. 我對政治不感興趣 。

This new method has been a great help to our industrial development. 這個新方法對我們的工業發展有很大的幫助 。

This ideology has greatly affected our nation's history. (i.e. This ideology in regard to our nation's history has had a great influence.) 這種思想對我國的歷史有很大的影響 。

**3.** *Guānyu* may be used to modify either a noun, pronoun or verb to give the meaning 'concerning', 'about' or 'regarding'.

I like to read novels about Chinese history. 我喜歡看關於中國歷史的小説 。

I often read books and magazines about scientific problems. 我常常看關於科學問題的書和雜誌 。

**4.** *Duìyu* and *guānyu* may be used with their objects as the topical subject of the sentence (hence stressing their objects) giving the meaning 'With regard to...' and 'As for...' respectively.

With regard to our industrial development, this problem is important. 對於我們的工業發展,這個問題很重要 。

As for (the matter of) your going to China this year, you will have to ask them. 關於你今年去中國的事,你得問他們 。

## Verbal Constructions in Sequence to Show Purpose or Means of an Action

Two or more verbal constructions in sequence may be used to show purpose e.g. 'I must go home to sleep' is *Wǒ yào huíjiā shuìjiào* 我要回家睡覺 。

*Lai* 來 or *qu* 去 are often used to connect a verbal construction of purpose with the verbal construction preceding it. *Lai* and *qu* may be used to indicate the purpose of coming or going but sometimes they may be used simply to introduce the second action without any implication of direction.

He came here to teach. 他到這兒來教書 。

He wants to go to China to study Chinese literature. 他想到中國去學中國文學 。

He sent three letters telling her to come back. 他寄了三封信去叫她回來 。

He did not use soap to wash his hands. 他没有用肥皂來洗手 。

## Conjunctions and Conjunctive Phrases

**1.** *Yòu* 又 ... *yòu* 又 ... is a construction used to connect parallel but different verbal or adjectival predicates or the adjectives of a complement of degree. Used with affirmative predicates the meaning 'both... and...' is conveyed. The negative form gives the meaning 'neither... nor...'.

This pen is both cheap and good. 這枝筆又便宜又好 。

She wrote the letter both quickly and well. 這封信,她寫得又快又好 。

He wanted both to cry and to laugh. 他又想哭,又想笑 。

**2.** *Chúle* 除了 ... (*yǐwài* 以外) means 'apart from' in both an inclusive and exclusive sense.

Inclusive: *Chúle... (yǐwài...) hái* 還 /*yě* 也 /*yòu* 又 gives the meaning of 'besides', 'in addition', 'as well as'.

Besides studying Chinese, I am studying Japanese. 除了學中文,我還學日文 。

Besides seeing a friend I want to go to the library to borrow books. 除了去看朋友,我還想去圖書館借書 。

As well as writing two letters I made three telephone calls. 除了寫兩封信,我又打了三次電話 。

Exclusive: *Chúle... (yǐwài...) dōu* 都 gives the meaning 'apart from', 'excluding'.

Apart from my younger sister we can all drive a car. 除了我妹妹,我們都會開車 。

Except for my younger brother we have all been to Beijing. 除了我弟弟,我們都去過北京 。

**3.** *Búdàn* 不但 ... *érqiě* 而且 ... means 'not only... but also...'. This construction is used to place stress on the relative importance of the predicate following *érqiě*.

Not only can he speak French but he can speak it extremely well. 他不但會説法語,而且説得很好 。

Not only did he wash them very slowly but he did not wash them clean. 他不但洗得很慢,而且洗得不乾淨 。

**4.** *Yuè* 越 ... *yuè* 越 ... means 'the more... the more...'.

The more he read, the more quickly he was able to read. 他書看得越多,看起來看得越快 。

The more he drank the sleepier he felt. 他酒喝得越多,越覺得想睡 。

**5.** *Yuè lái yuè* 越來越 … means 'increasingly…', 'more and more…' or in its negative form 'less and less…'. My books became increasingly numerous. 我的書 越來越多。

This type of wine is getting more and more expensive. 這種酒越來越貴。

**6.** *Bù* 不 …*bù* 不 … means '(if) not… not…', 'not… unless…'

If you do not tell him, he won't know. 如果你不 告訴他，他不會知道。

I shall not go unless you go. 你不去,我就不去。

**7.** *Yìbiānr* 一邊兒… *yìbiānr* 一邊兒… means '(doing something) while at the same time (doing something else)'.

She is singing while washing the clothes. 她一邊兒 洗衣服，一邊兒唱歌。

She is weeping as she reads the novel. 她一邊兒 看小說，一邊兒哭。

**8.** *Jìrán* 既然…*jiù* 就/*nàme* 那麼…. means 'since/as… then…'. This construction is used with a causal clause to express a known reason.

Since he has arrived we can begin to eat. 他既然來 了，我們就可以開始吃飯了。

Since he did not dare to do it himself, I did it for him. 他既然不敢自己做，我就給他做了。

**9.** *Yàoshi* 要是/*yào* 要/*jiǎrú* 假如 … *jiù* 就… means 'if… then…'. This construction is used to express condition. It should be noted that *yàoshi/yào/jiǎrú* may be omitted as *jiù* alone can express condition. Also, when *yàoshi/yào/jiǎrú* is used, *jiù* may be omitted if there is an adverbial modifier e.g. *yídìng* 一定, *yě* 也 in the second clause.

If you do not go then I will not go. 假如你不去, 我就不去。

If you go then he will also go. 要是你去，他也 就去。

If you do not go home immediately he is certain to be angry. 你要是不立刻回家，他一定會生 氣。

If you do not buy it for him then I shall. 你要不 給他買，我就給他買。

**10.** *Chúfēi* 除非 … *yàoburán* 要不然 … means 'not… unless…'.

Unless you help me I shall not be able to do it well. 除非你幫助我，要不然我就弄不好。

I shall not be able to finish doing it unless you help me. 除非你幫我忙，要不然我就做不完。

**11.** *Chúfēi* 除非 …*cái* 才… means 'only if… will then…'.

Only a child would write a letter like that. 除非是 小孩子，才會寫一封這樣的信。

Only if he doesn't know will he not come. 除非他 不知道，他才會不來。

**12.** *Zhǐyào* 只要 … *jiù* 就… means 'provided that', 'so long as… then…'. This is a construction used with clauses to express necessary condition.

Provided that you go in the morning you will certainly be able to see him. 只要你早上去，你就一定 能見到他。

As long as you write him a letter he will immediately come. 只要你寫一封信給他，他就會立 刻來。

**13.** *Búshi* 不是… *jiùshi* 就是… means 'if not… then…'.

If these things are not his then they belong to the teacher. 這些東西不是他的，就是老師 的。

If you do not go, then he will go. 不是你去，就 是他去。

**14.** *Jì* 既… *yòu* 又 /*érqiě* 而且 … means 'both… and…'. This construction is used to place equal emphasis on both elements.

He came early and moreover brought the money. 他既來得早，又把錢拿來了。

He came late and moreover forgot to do the shopping. 他既來得晚，又忘了買東西。

**15.** (*Suīrán* 雖然)… *yě* 也 /*kěshi* 可是 /*dànshi* 但是 means '(although)… yet…'. The use of *suīrán* is optional in this construction.

He is very slow but does not write even one character incorrectly. 他雖然很慢，可是一個字也 不會寫錯。

Although I looked for three days I still could not find it. 我雖然找了三天，也找不到。

**16.** *Yīnwei* 因為 … *suóyi* 所以 … means 'because… therefore…'. Either *yīnwei* or *suóyi* may be omitted, or if the meaning is clear both may be omitted. Note that the reason or cause clause comes first. *Yīnwei* is followed by a verbal expression or a full subject + predicate clause. The verbal forms *wèile* 為了 and *wèizhe* 為 着 are used for nominal expressions.

I did not go because he did not tell me. 因為他沒 有告訴我，所以我沒有去。

I do not have the money to buy a house because I cannot find work. 因為我找不到工作，所以我 沒有錢買房子。

**17.** *Zhèng yīnwei* 正因為… *suóyi* 所以… means 'it is precisely because… that…'.

It is precisely because I cannot find work that I cannot buy those books. 正因為我找不到工作，所 以我不能買那些書。

It is precisely because he did not return that the work has not been finished. 正因為他沒回來，所以 工作還沒做完呢。

**18.** *Jiùshi* 就是/*jíshǐ* 即使… *yě* 也/*dōu* 都/*hái* 還 means 'even if… still…'.

*Jiùshi* or *jíshǐ* is used in the qualifying clause and an

# NOTES ON GRAMMAR

adverb with the meaning 'still' is used in the main clause.
Even if he does not dare to go, I dare to. 就是他
不敢去，我也敢去。
Even if you will not tell me I still have ways of finding
out. 即使你不肯告訴我，我還有辦法
知道。

**19.** *Gāng* 剛… *jiù* 就… means 'just as… then…'. This
construction is used for immediately successive or con-
temporaneous events that have no causal connections.
I had just finished eating when they arrived. 我剛吃
完，他們就來了。
I had just sat down when they ran in. 我剛坐下，
他們就跑進來了。

**20.** *Bùguǎn* 不管/*búlùn* 不論/*wúlùn* 無論… means 'no
matter… (still)…'. In this construction *bùguǎn/búlùn/
wúlùn* are used at the beginning of a qualifying clause
and followed by an adverb such as *yě* 也 or *hái* 還 which
gives the meaning 'still' in the main clause.
No matter how much money you have you will not be
able to buy it. 不管你有多少錢，也買不到。
No matter how well you speak Japanese you will still not
be able to speak it as well as him. 不論你的日語
說得多麼好，你還是沒有他說得好。